Joseph Cook and Co.

Report Presented at the Annual Meeting of the Seventeeth

Anniversary

Of the New South Wales Instituition for the Deaf and Dumb an the Blind...

Joseph Cook and Co.

Report Presented at the Annual Meeting of the Seventeeth Anniversary
Of the New South Wales Instituition for the Deaf and Dumb an the Blind...

ISBN/EAN: 9783744763288

Printed in Europe, USA, Canada, Australia, Japan

Cover: Foto ©ninafisch / pixelio.de

More available books at **www.hansebooks.com**

REPORT

PRESENTED AT THE

ANNUAL MEETING OF THE SEVENTEENTH ANNIVERSARY

OF THE

New South Wales Institution

FOR THE

DEAF AND DUMB AND THE BLIND,

For the Year Ending 30th September, 1878,

WITH

THE TREASURER'S BALANCE SHEETS,

LISTS OF DONATIONS AND SUBSCRIPTIONS,

AND

Information Concerning the Admission of Children.

Sydney:
JOSEPH COOK & CO., PRINTERS, 370, GEORGE STREET,
OPPOSITE THE BANK OF NEW SOUTH WALES.

1878.

3

LIFE DIRECTORS.

3

APPOINTED UNDER RULE IV.

Clause 3.

KING, REV. GEORGE, M.A. | ROBINSON, F. R., ESQ.
LOVE, WILLIAM, ESQ., J.P.

Clause 4.

ROBINSON, ELLIS, ESQ. | PHILLIPS, H., ESQ.

Clause 5.

LANG, REV. DR. | FRAZER, JOHN, ESQ., J.P.
BEILBY, E. T., ESQ. | HILLS, ROBERT, ESQ.
HENRY, JAMES, ESQ. | FAIRFAX, JAMES R., ESQ.
MILNE, REV. JAMES.

Clause 6.

BELMORE, His Excellency The Right Hon. Earl of
PAXTON, JOSEPH, ESQ. | WALKER, THOMAS, ESQ.
HOLTERMANN, B. O., ESQ. | CAMPBELL, W. B., ESQ.

Clause 7.

JOY, EDWARD, ESQ. | WISE, GEORGE F., ESQ.

Names of Donors of £50 and upwards in aid of the Funds of the Institution.

His Excellency the Right Hon. Earl of Belmore. Donations £350.

Fairfax and Sons ...Donation £100	William Keel ... Bequest 150
Mrs. Mary Roberts ,, 100	John W. Wood ... Donation 100
James Williams ... Bequest 100	B. O. Holtermann ,, 100
Maurice Alexander ,, 50	Joseph Paxton, J.P. ,, 50
Dr. Charles Muller ... Don. 100	Hamilton Hume ... Bequest 50
Hon. John Frazer ... ,, 50	William Moffitt... ,, 250
Bryan Fall ... ... Bequest 50	Hugh Nolan... ... ,, 100
Thomas Walker ... Donation 200	Thomas Frost ... ,, 100
John W. Wood ... Bequest 1000	Button Charles ... ,, 50
Mrs. Sarah White ,, 50	F. H. Dangar ... Donation 50
William Manson ... ,, 1000	Richard Slee ... ,, 50

RESOLUTIONS passed at the Seventeenth Annual Meeting, held at the INSTITUTION, Newtown Road, on MONDAY AFTERNOON, 14th October, 1878.

SIR JOHN HAY, K.C.B., M.L.C., &c., &c., in the Chair.

Moved by the REV. GEORGE KING, M.A.
Seconded by WILLIAM FOWLER, ESQ., J.P.:—
"That the Report now read be adopted, and, together with the balance-sheet be printed for circulation." Carried unanimously.

Moved by the REV. DR. STEEL,
Seconded by MR. G. F. WISE :—
"That the thanks of this Meeting are hereby given to the Government and Parliament for the annual donation of £450, in aid of the funds of the Institution." Carried unanimously.

Moved by MR. JOHN DAVIES, M.P.,
Seconded by MR. F. R. ROBINSON :—
"That the following gentlemen do constitute the Committee for the ensuing year :—*President*, the Rev. George King, M.A. ; *Vice-President*, Rev. James Milne, M.A. ; *Hon. Treasurer*, Mr. Henry Phillips ; *Hon. Secretary*, Mr. Ellis Robinson ; *Hon. Surgeon*, Mr. Arthur Renwick, M.D. ; *Committee*, Mr. E. T. Beilby, Mr. S. C. Brown, M.L.A., Hon. John Frazer, M.L.C., Mr. J. R. Fairfax, Mr. Robert Hills, Mr. James Henry, Mr. J. R. Linsley, J.P., Mr. F. R. Robinson, Mr. George F. Wise, Mr. J. R. Love, Mr. Joseph Paxton, Mr. E. Saber, Mr. John Mills." Carried unanimously.

SEVENTEENTH ANNUAL REPORT

OF THE

NEW SOUTH WALES

Institution for the Deaf & Dumb, & the Blind.

For the Year ending September 30th, 1878.

The Committee in presenting to the Subscribers and the Public their Report of the Twelve months work, have again the pleasure of congratulating all concerned on the very satisfactory position of the Institution.

The year just ended has been an eventful one for the Institution, and the first subject claiming attention, is the

PROGRESS OF THE PUPILS.

This has been satisfactory, though perhaps somewhat checked through Mr. Watson's absence in England for seven months. The new books for the Blind mentioned in last report, were received shortly after the holding of the Annual Meeting, and found of great benefit.

The Annual Examination was held on December 22nd last, and as usual, Prizes were distributed.

HEALTH OF THE PUPILS.

Has been unusually good. Dr. Renwick's services as before having been freely given. The appearance of the Children indicates the care and attention bestowed upon them. It may be opportune here to draw attention to a matter of great importance—viz., the erection of a *Detached Hospital,* for the use of the children, and for isolation, should any epidemic arise. The Committee, after serious consideration, have finally decided to carry out this object, and the Fund at their disposal, now amounting to £850, has been devoted towards this highly necessary work.

Number of Inmates.

The last report showed that there were 70 Inmates, and 5 have been admitted since, (4 Deaf and Dumb, 1 Blind,) making a total of 75. 14 of these have left, some to go to Trades, others to their Friends; all having received an incalculable advantage during their stay in the Institution.

Applications for the admission of 6 have been granted, but the children have not yet been received; and several applications are pending further particulars being forwarded.

Financial.

The amount of Subscriptions, &c., has increased £271 6s. 9d. The country receipts being as usual satisfactory, and the Committee have again to tender their thanks for the substantial assistance which has been afforded. The Balance last year was £130 14s. 5d., in addition to £300 applied towards the erection of the Dwarf Wall and Railings.

The Government grant for 1877, was not received in time to be included in last years financial statement; consequently two grants appear in the Balance Sheet now presented.

The increased amount of Receipts enable the Committee to appropriate £850 towards the erection of the intended Hospital.

Early in the year it was found impossible for the sole Collector to canvass thoroughly this Colony and Queensland; consequently a second Collector, Mr. W. B. Stevens, was appointed for Queensland. He has collected £400 and discovered the existence of 8 or 9 Deaf and Dumb and Blind Children; 5 of whom he will bring with him on his return, and the others will probably come in due course. The appointment of Mr. Stevens has turned out an advantage in this respect, and he has also visited the Friends of some of the Children, awakening greater interest, and securing an increased amount of support in Queensland for the 18 Children received from that Colony.

The Special Receipts and Donations, are as under—

Legacy of Mr. William Dale, per Rev. Canon Stephen	£100	0	0
,, Mrs. Sarah White, per Hon. James White	50	0	0
., William Barnett, per Mr. George Merriman	40	0	0
,, William Quinn, per Shepherd Smith, Esq.	25	0	0
,, Jean Malcolm	6	1	8

Donation of F. H. Dangar, Esq.	.. ..	£50	0	0
,, Richard Sloe, Esq...	.. ..	50	0	0
Collection—Mr. A. Thomas, Queensland Railway Line		33	4	0
,, Gerringong Municipal Council	.. ..	35	2	0
,, Mr. W. G. O'Neil ..	.. ..	31	4	6

And other smaller amounts. One Bequest deserves special notice, not from the amount, but the feelings which prompted it; this is 14s., the whole earthly possession of a Prisoner who died in East Maitland Gaol.

The Receipts for School Fees and Clothing, amount to £482 13s. 10d., as against £563 19s. last year, showing a decrease of £81 5s. 2d. There is yet some School Fees due from the parents of children in the country, but the bad seasons have hindered them paying promptly.

IMPROVEMENTS AND ADDITIONS.

The erection of the Dwarf Wall rendered some additional planting of Shade Trees desirable. This has been completed through the kindness of Mr. Charles Moore, Director of the Botanical Gardens. A large amount of Fencing has also been erected.

GENERAL.

The Committee have to express their deep regret at the loss the Institution has sustained by the death of the Rev. Dr. Lang, who took an active part for so many years in its management, and worked zealously for its welfare. The Committee immediately after the sad event, sent a letter of condolence and sympathy to his bereaved family.

The Committee take this opportunity of acknowledging the valuable assistance so cheerfully given by the Press of this Colony and Queensland, and the readiness displayed in furthering the work of the Collectors by notices and paragraphs inserted gratuitously.

It is also here the Committee have to acknowledge many other kind and valuable services. Among them the Picnic given the Children and Officers by Lady Hay, at her residence. The invitation to the Newtown Sunday School Picnic, per Mr. Crane; and the Collection at St. Ann's Church, Ryde, per the Churchwardens, for a Treat to the Children; as also Mr. Seymour, for frequent Donations of Fresh Fish; Mr. Wigzell, Hair cutting.

8

The Committee have now to refer to the visit of Mr. Watson to Great Britain and America. Mr. Watson, finding his seven years residence in the Institution and the arduous character of his work had rendered a change desirable, applied for leave of absence to visit Europe, and at the same time to enquire into all the newest and most advanced methods of imparting instruction to the Deaf and Dumb and the Blind; also to obtain a supply of the most modern appliances and apparatus. Accordingly, the Committee granted the leave applied for, and have the pleasure to report Mr. Watson's safe return after having devoted the greater portion of his time to the purpose above set forth; he has returned with renewed strength and energy to his duties, having acquired much information in England, Scotland, Ireland and America. He has also purchased, and otherwise obtained, a splendid assortment of Books and Material, a small portion of which is now in the Harbour, and the remainder will shortly arrive.

The Committee desire to acknowledge most gratefully, the very kind assistance and valuable help given to Mr. Watson by the Managers of the numerous Institutions he visited, and the courteous manner in which he was every where received. They have also to thank many kinds friends for Donations of Books, &c., &c.

In accordance with the Rules, the following Gentlemen have been appointed Life Directors, viz., Mr. James R. Fairfax, Rev. James Milne, M.A., Dr. A. Renwick, Mr. James Henry and Mr. Robert Hills. The Rev. James Milne has also been appointed Vice-President in room of the late Dr. Lang.

CONCLUSION.

In conclusion, the Committee have to report the Institution in a very flourishing condition, the health of the Children good, and the whole Establishment in such a state that they may consider this Report one of the most satisfactory and encouraging they have had the pleasure of yet placing before the public. They now commend the Institution and its inmates to the care of that Divine Providence who "ordereth all things for good." And to Him they offer their heartfelt thanks for the success attending their efforts.

G. KING. *President.*

ELLIS ROBINSON, *Hon. Secretary.*

September 30th, 1878.

Visit of Royal Commissioners on Charitable Institutions.

The gentlemen appointed as a Royal Commission to report upon the charities of the colony, paid a visit of inspection in due course to this Institution, and in their most exhaustive and able report notified their impressions as being most satisfactory, and the following extract from the Second Report of the Commissioners appointed to inquire into, and report upon, the Working and Management of the Public Charities of the Colony, 29th May, 1874, page 117 :—

"The Institution for the Deaf and Dumb and the Blind.—This Institution being to a small extent assisted by a Parliamentary vote, we made an inquiry into its management. We found it contained Twenty-one Deaf and Dumb Boys, and an equal number of Girls of the same class, besides Five Blind Boys and Seven Blind Girls, 54 in all. The management appeared to us to be good, and we remarked nothing calling for particular notice. The institution is conducted on unsectarian principles, and from its truly charitable character, is in every way deserving of public support."

The Following is the Report Presented to the Government and Parliament by the Inspector of Charities.

The Inspector of Charities reports of this Institution as follows :—

"This very popular and truly charitable institution is subsidized by Government only to the extent of £450, and is under the control of its own elected board and directory.

The objects set forth in its prospectus are to educate and maintain children deaf and dumb or blind, to enable them to earn their own living, make them useful members of society, and prevent them becoming burdensome to others in after life.

In order to enlarge the sphere of its operations, render the internal administration more economical, and so increase its means for imparting a thoroughly good system of education, the directors decided on admitting on certain conditions into the institution children from the neighbouring colonies of Queensland, Tasmania, and New Zealand, where to the present time no institutions of similar character exist. Among these conditions are two, viz. :—

1st. That a guarantee be given that a child on leaving the institution shall be conveyed to its own colony.

2nd. That its cost while in the school shall be paid by responsible parties to the extent of £25 per annum.

When obtainable, the above sum of £25 is always demanded, but pauper children residing in this colony are received free, and in cases where the parents or guardians cannot command the full sum, less is accepted after due inquiry.

No child is eligible under seven years of age, nor excepting in special cases, beyond twelve years.

As education can only be received slowly, owing to physical disability, pupils may continue in the institution until the age of eighteen. In the great majority of cases, however, they leave much earlier—say at fifteen or sixteen years old.

No trades are taught, experience in similar institutions elsewhere tending to show that it is preferable to confine the attention of pupils to their mental cultivation, leaving handicrafts to be acquired afterwards as apprentices, in ordinary workshops. I have not myself collected sufficient evidence to express any opinion as to the correctness of this theory, but in practical working the plan is unavoidable so long as the numbers to be taught are very limited, as at present is the case.

The domestic work of the establishment is all done by the pupils (the deaf mutes). The blind who show talent are taught music, with a view to its becoming a means of livelihood.

The conduct of such an institution has of course to be peculiar, and is in some respects necessarily expensive. The management appears excellent, and has the advantage of a ladies' committee, which works harmoniously with the matron of the institution. The children look clean and well cared for, happy and contented. As may be expected both from the slowness of its inception and the wide difference in the ages at which the pupils severally begin their education, the classes are very irregular. I observed also a considerable diversity of intellectual strength in the children.

A summary of the working of the institution from its foundation may be found in the following note, transcribed from the last published annual report :—

To 30th September last, there have been 131 children received—112 deaf and dumb and 19 blind ; 60 have been returned : 6 were found idiotic and beyond the influence of education—these were removed to asylums for the insane ; 1 died ; 66 remained at date in the school. In 15 families, two or more were deaf mutes. 108 came from New South Wales, 17 from Queensland, 2 from New Zealand, 3 from Tasmania, and 1 from South Australia.

The balance-sheet for the year 1874 shows that the public subscribed a sum of £1428 18s. 9d., and that a further amount of £453 1s. 9d. was received for school fees and clothing. This is in most favourable contrast to the results shown by most of our other charitable institutions, where the difference between respective amounts of subscriptions and payments as compared with the Government subsidy is very discouraging.

Composition by the Pupils.

The following specimens of composition, or essays are the work of some of the elder pupils, (the subjects are of their own choosing) and receive no correction except such as their respective writers can make on a careful review, when the prominent errors are pointed out by a Teacher. In judging them it is well to remember the ages of the writers, and the length of time at school. And that very few, if any, had acquired a knowledge of written or spoken language previously to their admission into the Institution.

By H. B.
ABOUT THE CONGRESS AT BERLIN.

The Congress was held last June at Berlin in Prussia. Prince Bismark was the chairman at it. Some gentlemen from England, France, Austria, and Russia met there. They talked about the war between Russia and Turkey. The Congress remained at Berlin for many days. We hope that war has ended, and that there will be peace. The Russians are urging the Afghans to fight against the English, Lord Beaconsfield returned to England with Lord Salisbury after the Congress at Berlin. The people heartily welcomed him and they gave many addresses to Lord Beaconsfield. The Afghans have fought against the English. I think the Russians wish to take India. They are very ambitious to take India. The Afghans are wild mountaineers. Afghanistan is north of India. The Afghan ruler is called the Ameer. Cyprus now belongs to England. It is an Island in the Mediterranean Sea. The English were very glad to get Cyprus into their possession. I never saw Afghanistan. I saw the picture of Lord Beaconsfield and Lord Salisbury's return to England.

By A. F.
ABOUT A VISIT TO ENGLAND.

Mr. —— went to England last February by the "Stadt Amsterdam." He stayed at Melbourne about five days and saw all about it. After that he went to Adelaide and then to Aden and Red Sea, touching at Suez, Port Said and Lisbon. He arrived in England safely on 3rd April. The "Stadt Amsterdam" went to England in about 63 days. He met his friends at home, and was very glad to see them. He went to see our dear friend Mr. Joy at the Isle of Wight. It lies south of Hampshire. It is a small but beautiful island. The ship touched at Plymouth. He stayed at home about 3 months, and then returned. He went from England to New York across the Atlantic Ocean. New York is a large and fine city. Afterwards he sat on the train and crossed America a distance of nearly 3000 miles. He passed over the Suspension bridge at the Falls of Niagara and saw the river Niagara. The train crossed the different bridges slowly. If it passed over very fast, the bridge would be broken and the people drowned in the river. He visisted Deaf and Dumb and Blind Institutions at New York and other places. He saw many pupils in it. Some pupils there go home for vacation to see their parents as we do. The population of New York is over 1,000,000. The population of San

Francisco is about 300,000. San Francisco is a large and growing city and there are many Chinese in it, also large hotels. He went from San Francisco to Auckland. He met John Selly who is a Deaf and Dumb saddler and who left School two years ago. He returned from Auckland to Sydney. He came to Sydney last September by the mail steamer Zealandia. He was very glad to see us I think.

By M. A. E.
ABOUT BELSHAZZAR.

Belshazzar was the grandson of Nebuchadnezzar and a bad King of Bablyon. He was fond of eating drinking and of worldly pleasures. A thousand bright lamps shone in the hall of Belshazzar and 1000 nobles were eating with him. He saw the hand writing on the wall. It was written "Mene mene Tekel Upharsin." He shook and felt terrified. He commanded the wise men to expound the words but they could not. His wife said unto him that Daniel was a good man and he could interpret the vision. Daniel came and said that Nebuchadnezzar had been a wicked King whose heart was hardened and full of pride. He was deposed from his kingly throne and driven from men and made like the beasts. They fed him with grass like oxen. His body was wet with the dew of heaven until he knew that God ruled in the kingdom of men. He became humble after this. "Mene means God hath numbered thy kingdom and finished it. Tekel means, Thou art weighed in the Balances and found wanting. Peres means Thy Kingdom is divided and given to the Medes and Persians. Cyrus came that night with an army and slew him. Darius was the new King of Babylon. Daniel was chosen as the Chief of the Presidents by Darius. The new King loved Daniel greatly and gave him a gold chain to put round his neck.

By C. J.
ABOUT OBEDIENCE.

Good persons love, obey, and fear God. The fifth commandment teaches us to obey our parents, teachers, magistrates, and others. "Honour thy father and thy mother that thy days may be long upon the land which the Lord thy God giveth thee." Paul says that, Children should obey their parents in the Lord, for this is right. Wicked children do not obey their parents. We read in the Bible about Absalom who was the son of David, and who dishonoured his father therefore God was angry with him and he was slain by Joab. God likes to see obedient and good people. God told Abraham that he should sacrifice his only son Isaac. Abraham obeyed God's command, for he had great faith. Peter told the Jewish Sanhedrim that he should obey God rather than man. God will bless obedient children. Jesus obeyed His parents. We should learn to be obedient at once. Many people are disobedient and bad, and do not obey God's commands. Paul says, "Wives should submit to their husbands. People should honor the King or governor. If children disobey their parents then God will be angry with them. They will be sent into hell. Eli's sons did not obey their father's Command, so they both died in battle against the Philistines. At first Paul obeyed the Jewish High priests in persecuting the christians, but he was converted on the way to Damascus. Samuel the prophet told King Saul that, "To obey is better than sacrifice. Saul had disobeyed God by not Killing Agag. Agag was a wicked King of Amalek. Adam and Eve disobeyed God by eating the forbidden fruit, so God drove them out of the garden of Eden. Nebuchadnezzar made a golden image and ordered all his subjects to worship it, but Shadrack, Meshack and Abednego refused to obey him, so they were cast into the fiery furnace at Babylon, but God preserved them.

SPEECHES AND PROCEEDINGS

SEVENTEENTH ANNUAL PUBLIC MEETING.

Extracted from the Daily Press.

The seventeenth annual meeting in connection with the New South Wales Institution for the Deaf and Dumb, and the Blind, was held in the Institution, Newtown Road, yesterday. The chair was occupied by Sir John Hay, M.L.C., and the hall in which the proceedings took place was crowded, principally with ladies. Amongst those present were the Revs. G. King, W. F. B. Uzzell, J. Milne, William Hough, Dr. Steel, J. Dark, the Hon. W. Marks, M.L.C.; Mr. John Davies, M.L.A., Messrs. W. Fowler, F. R. Robinson, H. Phillips, James Henry, G. F. Wise, D. A. Thomas, J. R. Love, E. Saber, Dr. Haylock, Dr. Renwick, Mrs. Holt, Mrs. Robinson, Mrs. Phillips, Mrs. Breillatt, Mrs. J. Watson, Mrs. Marks, Mrs. Renwick, Mrs. Goodlet, Lady Hay, and others.

After some of the inmates had given a few manifestations of their vocal and instrumental abilities.

The CHAIRMAN explained the object of their meeting. He said, also, that he desired to call the attention of those present to a very important matter in connection with that and similar institutions. Mr. Watson, their superintendent, lately had leave of absence, both for the purpose of recruiting his health and to obtain information as to the improved methods of teaching the deaf and dumb and blind in England some parts of Europe, and America. That gentleman had returned, and brought with him a pamphlet containing questions and answers in connection with the vexed question discussed some time ago, and still undecided, as to whether they were in the right track in using signs or finger language in the instruction of the inmates of the institution, or whether they should put those systems in the background and favour teaching the mute children to communicate with each other, and with people endowed with ordinary senses and faculties, by means of articulation or observation of the lips. He explained that the system of teaching by articulation was not a novelty as was generally supposed, and affirmed that it had been in use in Germany and some parts of the Austrian dominions for some considerable time, where it was thought preferable to the sign and finger language system. It had also been in use in some institutions in Great Britain, and was amongst the earliest plans adopted for enabling mutes to converse. One of the ablest authorities on the subject wrote, as far back as 1690, of the mode

of using the system of articulation, in the following quaint terms :—
" My first care is to make him to sound forth a voice without which
all labour is lost, but that one point whereby deaf persons do dis-
cern a voice from a mute breath is a great mystery of art, and
it is the hearing of deaf persons, or at least equivalent thereto,
viz., that trembling motion and titillation which they perceive in
their own throat, whilst they of their own accord do give out a
voice. That the deaf may know that I intend to give out a voice
I put their hand to my throat that they may be sensible of that
tremulous motion when I utter my voice; then I put the same hand
of theirs to their own throat and command them to imitate me ; nor am
I discouraged if their voice is hard and difficult, for in time it becomes
more and more polite." That described pretty fairly the first steps
towards teaching the deaf and dumb to speak ; and they know also
that, in the celebrated school at Bermondsey, recourse was had to the
system for teaching some of the most prominent pupils there. In other
institutions in England, and indeed in some parts of France, he said the
greatest reliance was placed on the system of teaching by signs and
finger language. So they had opportunities of comparing the results
of two systems. The German system, he stated had been taken up by
the wealthy, and no doubt great good would result from their efforts ;
but it was necessary that they should hesitate before adopting a system
which had not proved a general success in England, and at the sacrifice
of what seemed to be an easy means for the deaf and dumb to communicate with their fellow-creatures. In order to place the matter a little
more clearly before those who took an interest in it, he would read what
he had set down concerning it as it at present stood :—There are two
distinct methods of teaching—first, that in which the sign language
and manual alphabet form the basis of instruction ; and second, that in
which articulation and lip-reading form the basis of instruction. In
both of these the written language of the country is also taught. The
former prevails in England, France, the United States, and in most
continental countries, except Germany and the Austrian dominions,
where the education of the deaf and dumb is undertaken directly by
the State and conducted on the second method. In most cases, however, whichever the basis of instruction, a combined system is adopted
more or less. In the one method with signs and finger reading as the
rule articulation and lip-reading are used for the semi-dumb, semi-deaf,
and for those of the congenitally deaf who have good capacities and
show an aptitude for learning. In the other method with articulation
and lip-reading as the rule, the sign language and finger reading are
used more or less as means to an end. In some of the private schools
in England, and in some large institutions which have lately come into
notice there, it is understood that the *pure* German system, as it is called
is adopted, by which the manual language and signs are entirely discouraged, and only articulation and lip-reading, in conjunction with
written language, retained. Perhaps the merits of the system may
be well expressed in the words of a very recent writer :—" It
would at first sight appear scarcely credible, without the guidance
of the sense of hearing, that any person would be able merely by
watching the position and actions of the organs of the voice, to utter

articulate sounds with any tolerable perfection. Experience, however, has shown that this accomplishment, though laborious and tedious of acquisition, is not attended with extreme difficulty. Great patience, perseverance, and kindness are qualifications necessary on the part of the teacher to ensure success in ordinary cases, and the degree of success will greatly depend on the number of children among whom the teacher has to divide his attention. A wide difference must ever be perceptible between the speech of the deaf and those who hear. This artificial speech is laborious and constrained. It frequently conveys the idea of pain as well as effort, and as it cannot be regulated by the ear of the speaker, it is often too loud, and generally monotonous, harsh, and discordant. It is often from this cause scarcely intelligible, except to those who are accustomed to its tones. The system of articulation and lip-reading prevails in the German schools, where the art has been cultivated with greater success than in England, which must be attributed to the adaptability of the German language to this peculiar mode of acquiring speech." He understood that their teacher, Mr. Watson, on seeing the results of the most famous establishments in London, in which the articulation and lip reading systems were carried out, had arrived at the conclusion, that a combined system of signs of finger language was the best. It must be considered however, that articulation might be made useful to many of the deaf and dumb when they grew up. It seemed to be a system which the wealthy might take advantage of, but it was their duty to see that poor deaf and dumb children were suitably instructed, and with the fifty inmates of their institution they could scarcely hope to carry the system on to perfection, seeing that one person was required for several years to teach it to every six children. That, however, ought not to prevent their teaching the children in the most perfect manner possible, and they must take care to have opportunities given for every deaf and dumb child amongst them to acquire all in the way of tuition they were capable of receiving. They were, he said, entitled to assistance from the Government to enable them to do that, but he would not ask for so much assistance as would lead the Government to suppose they should have control of the institution, because, to his mind, it would not then thrive so well as it did under existing arrangements. As the State, however, was bound to provide for the education of every child, it was reasonable to suppose that it should, to some extent, provide for the education of the inmates of the institution. He concluded by saying that there was another institution for the blind which demanded their sympathies. It was situated in Boomerang-street, and, unfortunately, had come to a standstill for want of funds. He was confident that if its position were properly placed before the public, the public would supplement the amount left by a benevolent gentleman for building the institution. It was intended to elevate some of the adult blind from their present position, to teach them trades, to assist them in finding employers, to form a temporary home for them, and a depôt where the goods they produced should be placed on sale. He would not detain them any longer, for he was convinced they had assembled to witness the performance of the children and the result of their training, rather than to hear long speeches.

Mr. Ellis Robinson, the secretary, then read the Report, to be found on previous pages.

Mr. HENRY PHILLIPS, the treasurer, then read the balance-sheet, showing the income of the institution during the year, inclusive of a balance from the previous twelve months, to be £3570 15s. 2d., and the expenditure £3547 6s. 1d., thus leaving a small credit balance amounting to £23 9s. 1d.

The Rev. GEORGE KING proposed the adoption of the report. He said the report was of such a satisfactory character that it needed no argument to recommend it to the approval of the meeting. The health of the pupils throughout the year was a subject of thankfulness to all of them. Their progress in the several branches of education in which they were instructed was highly encouraging, and their general conduct deserving of all praise. Even during the absence of Mr. Watson, they seemed to feel that a new responsibility rested on themselves, and they did not disappoint the expectation of their friends. He visited the school occasionally, and always found them orderly and attentive. Mr. Watson, during his six month's absence on leave, utilised his holiday for the benefit of the institution, by obtaining fresh information on the improvements which have recently been introduced into the schools for the deaf and dumb and the blind in England and America, and they were happy to welcome him back again. He paid much attention to the system of articulation, as compared with that of the manual alphabet and signs, and the result of his experience was that for those deaf mutes, who in early life possessed the power of articulation in any degree it was indeed the greatest boon. But the great majority of the deaf and dumb suffered from a defect in the organs of voice, which rendered it a very long and tedious process, and in many instances an impossibility to teach them articulation. On the other hand, the manual alphabet came within the reach of all deaf mutes. Through this silent language they could readily be taught to converse, to read and write, and the ordinary course of school education. The manual alphabet was reliable and expressive, and the signs used were quicker than speech. For instance, if soldiers were the subject, touch the shoulder where epaulets were, and they understood it immediately. In fact, the manual alphabet and articulation were two distinct systems, each adapted for a separate class of deaf mutes; therefore, there should be no antagonism between them. They accepted both, and used both, methods. At the present time they had a class in the institution which had been under instruction in articulation for upwards of two years, and some of the pupils had made considerable progress in that system, as they should presently witness. He would take the present opportunity of correcting a mistake into which many visitors to the institution had fallen, and who had represented the institution as being only an educational school, and not embracing any trade instruction. This mistake arose from the absence of workshops in connection with the building. It should be known, however, that when youths come of age to learn a trade, they apprenticed them out, and had them taught at a tradesman's workshop. In that way five of their young men had been taught trades, and were now able to maintain themselves by the labour of their own hands; and the girls were all taught dressmaking and the use of the sewing machine, as well as all household work. That was all that could be done at present in the way of trades, and that had been accomplished for the last four years with success. He was desirous of having a workshop erected on a small scale, and of an inexpensive kind They would then be enabled to retain their young men who had learned trades, and utilise their acquirements for the benefit of the junior pupils. Thus when a boy had learned a trade, he would be able to impart it to all the others competent to learn it. That might also contribute something towards rendering the institution self-supporting. The committee also had in contemplation the erection of a hospital, but whether it should be detached or connected with the building was a question demanding very serious consideration. He would desire to commend their interesting cause to the earnest attention of the philanthropic public. He believed there was no other object which possessed a stronger and a purer claim on the affections of a charitable community. The loss of hearing and of speech on the one hand, and the deprivation of sight on the other, presented to their contemplation the saddest and gloomiest phases of human life, which their imagination was capable of conceiving. The deaf and dumb were shut out by nature from all communion with their fellow men ; the sources of moral and intellectual perception were cut off from them, and consequently their mind was sealed in darkness, and their life remained a blank. To the blind on the other hand, the whole book of nature, with her exquisite beauty, her sublime lessons of transcendental knowledge, and her glorious illustrations of the character and attributes of the great Creator of all things, was closed, and sealed, and placed beyond their reach for ever. The sun by day to them was darkened, and the moon and stars by night were blotted out of the sky. The bright verdure of nature's beautiful carpet, her sweet and lovely flowers which beamed upon other people's souls with smiles from heaven ; her rich and glowing landscape, with all its grand and charming variety, have never spoken to their soul, never stirred up within their breast one emotion of pleasure or enjoyment. Their whole life was one long, weary, solitary night, the blackness of darkness resting upon it. And all this without any fault of their own, or of their parents. "Who did sin ?" asked the caviller of old, " this man or his parents, that he was born blind ?" Mark the Divine reply, " Neither has this man sinned nor his parents, but that the works of God might be made manifest in him." Let them manifest then the works of God by the kind attention and tender care which they had it in their power to bestow on these, his afflicted children. God had given them an opportunity of repairing the deficiencies of nature by the new organs of sight, of hearing, and of speech, which the institution supplied. They cannot accomplish that themselves ; but they could contribute to the good work by giving generously of the means with which God had blessed them. They might thus become the honoured instruments of enabling the friends of the institution to carry on their hallowed work to completion, and bring down a blessing on their own heads.

Mr. WILLIAM FOWLER seconded the proposition with much pleasure, and, on being put, it was agreed to unanimously.

The Rev. Dr. STEEL moved,—" That the thanks of this meeting are hereby given to the Government and Parliament for the annual donation of £450, in aid of the funds of the institution."

Mr. G. F. Wise seconded the resolution, which was agreed to.

Mr. John Davies then moved,—" That the following gentlemen do constitute the committee for the ensuing year :—President, the Rev. George King, M.A. ; vice-president, Rev. James Milne ; hon. treasurer, Mr. Henry Phillips ; hon secretary, Mr. Ellis Robinson ; hon. surgeon, Mr. Arthur Renwick, M.D. ; committee, Mr. E. T. Beilby, Mr. S. C. Brown, M.L.A., Hon. John Frazer, M.L C., Mr. J. R. Fairfax, Mr. Robert Hills, Mr. James Henry, Mr. J. R. Linsley, J.P., Mr. F. R. Robinson, Mr. George F. Wise, Mr. J. R. Love, Mr. Joseph Paxton, Mr. E. Saber, Mr. John Mills."

This was duly seconded by Mr. F. R. Bobinson, and carried unanimously.

After this Mr. Watson, the superintendent, gave a brief address on the system of teaching mutes to communicate with each other by lip reading, and introduced some of the inmates of the institution for the purpose of practically illustrating the method. These proceedings were regarded with a great deal of interest by those present, and seemed fairly perfect as far as they went. Some blind children then read from embossed books, and others gave proofs of their vocal and musical abilities by playing the piano or singing. Several mutes gave exhibitions of their power to express by signs their feelings to each other, and after the National Anthem had been sung by the children and the audience, the visitors dispersed to have a look over the Institution, or to examine the plain and fancy needlework, knitting, &c., done by some of its inmates.

In the evening the children were given a treat by Mrs. M. Metcalfe.

Sydney, 30th September, 1878.

HENRY PHILLIPS, Hon. Treasurer in a/c with N.S.W. Institution for the Deaf & Dumb, & the Blind.

GENERAL FUND ACCOUNT.

Dr.	Income.	£	s.	d.		Cr.	Expenditure.	£	s.	d.
	To Balance at credit in Commercial Bank as per last years account	130	14	5			By Salaries, Labour, &c.	833	8	11
	,, Subscriptions and Donations (public)	851	16	3			,, Provisions, Groceries, and fodder for Cow	329	18	6
	,, Amount received for School Fees	420	5	0			,, Furniture, additions, fencing, alterations, repairs, &c.	294	18	3
	,, Re-payments for Clothing by Parents	62	8	10			,, Drapery, Clothing, Boots, Bedding, &c.	174	1	0
	,, Amount of Collections in (N. S. W.) Country Districts by Mr. Luff, as per lists	626	14	6			,, Fuel, lighting, and medicine	56	10	1
	,, ditto ditto in Queensland Districts by Mr. Stevens, Second Collector as per lists	320	16	0			,, Advertising, printing, stationery, and printing annual report	143	18	4
	,, Grant from N. S. Wales Government for 1877	450	0	0			,, Sundries, petty house expenses, &c.	75	14	4
	,, ,, ,, ,, 1878	450	0	0			,, Commission, travelling allowances, collecting expenses, stamps, &c.	446	1	3
	,, Interest on Investment of J. W. Wood's Legacy	47	1	7			,, Books for Blind, &c., Desks & School requisites	43	0	5
	,, Amount received for sale of frames	0	7	0			,, Insurance on Buildings and Furniture	4	15	0
	,, Contents of Visitors Box at the Institution	4	12	3			,, Transfer to Building Fund Account for railing, &c.	100	0	0
	,, "Samaritan" boxes	5	1	8			,, Paid half premium for boy Saunders apprenticed to chair caning	5	0	0
	,, Amount Collected by W. G. O'Neil, Queanbeyan	31	4	6			,, Amount appropriated for erection of detached hospital	850	0	0
	,, ,, E. Armitage, Maryboro	5	12	6			,, Balance, being amount at credit in Commercial Bank	23	9	1
	,, ,, Master McIntyre, Tinonee	12	17	0						
	,, Amount Donation from Geringong Municipality	35	2	0						
	,, Donation received from W. Bull	10	0	0						
	,, Legacy, Estate W. Dale, per Canon Stephen	100	0	0						
	,, ,, from Jean Malcom's Estate	6	1	8						
		£3,570	15	2				£3,570	15	2
	To Balance brought down, being Amount at credit of Account in Commercial Bank	£23	9	1						

Audited and found correct, 8 Oct., 1878.

JOHN F. PAIGE, } Auditors.
W. H. MACKENZIE, SEN. }

E. & O. E., Sydney, 30th September, 1878.

HENRY PHILLIPS, Hon. Treasurer.

Sydney, 30th September, 1878.

HENRY PHILLIPS, *Hon. Treasurer, in a/c with* N.S.W. INSTITUTION FOR THE DEAF & DUMB, & THE BLIND.

BUILDING FUND ACCOUNT.

Dr.   **Cr.**

INCOME.	£	s.	d.	EXPENDITURE.	£	s.	d.
To Balance of last year's account in Commercial Bank	19	18	5	By Payments to Contractor for Iron Railing and Gates, and Dwarf Wall	201	11	6
" Legacy received from the late B. Barnet's Exors.	40	0	0	" Architect's Commission on same and previous contract	47	12	0
" Ditto ditto William Quinn's Executors	25	0	0				
" Donation received from Mr. R. Slee, in trust for Ladies Committee	50	0	0				
" Transfer from General Fund Account	100	0	0				
" Balance, being overdraft at Commercial Bank	14	5	1				
	£249	3	6		£249	3	6
				By Balance brought down, being amount of over-draft at Commercial Bank	£14	5	1

Audited and found correct, 8 Oct. 1878.
JOHN F. PAIGE,
W. H. MACKENZIE, Sen. } *Auditors.*

E. & O. E., Sydney, 30th September, 1878.
HENRY PHILLIPS, *Hon. Treasurer.*

PERPETUAL SUBSCRIBERS' FUND ACCOUNT.

Dr.   **Cr.**

TRUSTEES—Rev. G KING, *President;* HENRY PHILLIPS, *Hon. Treasurer;* ELLIS ROBINSON, *Hon. Secretary.*

	£	s.	d.		£	s.	d.
To Amount Legacy received from the Estate of the late John W. Wood, of Globe Point..	1,000	0	0	By Purchase of N. S. W. 5 per cent. Debentures—			
				One of............ £500 0 0			
				Four each of £100............ 400 0 0	900	0	0
				" Premium paid on same 6¼ per cent............	58	10	0
				" Balance deposited in Savings Bank to credit of the Institution as per Pass Book............	41	10	0
	£1,000	0	0		£1,000	0	0

Audited and found correct, 8 Oct. 1878.
JOHN F. PAIGE,
W. H. MACKENZIE, Sen. } *Auditors.*

E. & O. E., Sydney, 30th September, 1878.
HENRY PHILLIPS, *Hon. Treasurer.*

Annual Subscriptions, Donations, &c.

Received for the year ending 30th September, 1878.

☞ N.B.—It is particularly requested that should any omission or inaccuracy appear in this list it be notified to the Secretary for correction.

GENERAL LIST.

	£	s.	d.
Ashcroft, James, Canonbar	1	0	0
Alexander, C.S., Goulburn J.P. 1877, C.P.S.	1	1	0
Anonymous, Langford Post Office	1	0	0
Abbey, W.	1	1	0
Albery and Co.	1	1	0
Alcock, Mrs., per Mrs. Hellier	1	1	0
Alexander, Mrs.	1	1	0
Abigail, F.	0	10	6
Anderson, James	0	10	0
Allen, Sir George Wigram	2	2	0
Ahronson, H., Cundletown	1	1	0
Aitken, T.	1	1	0
Anderson and Co.	1	1	0
Allt and Co.	1	1	0
Ash, F., Newcastle	1	1	0
Ash, W., Singleton	1	1	0
Ash, J., Newcastle	1	0	0
Atherden, George	2	0	0
Allan, H. E. A.	1	0	0
Atkinson, George, 1877	1	1	0
Alger, J.	1	1	0
Atkinson, George	1	1	0
Allerding, F. and Son	1	1	0
Allen, Rev. D.	1	1	0
Barnetts Legacy, B. Barnett Executor	40	0	0
Backhouse, B.	£2	2	0
Bucknell, W. W., Cook's River	2	0	0
Brocklehurst, W. W., London, per Wolfen & Co.	5	0	0
Biss, Mrs. H., Quarterly	1	0	0
Boucher, J., Cooma	1	1	0
Bryce, Rev. J. G., Braidwood	1	1	0
Brodribb, Mrs., per Lady Hay	1	1	0
Bailey, W., Bequest, per R. A. Stace	0	14	0
Boyd, Adam, J.P , Broughton Creek	1	0	0
Bonynge, T., Wagga Wagga	1	1	0
Buchanan, B.	2	2	0
Baylis, E.	0	10	0
Binnie, R.	2	2	0
Berry, D., "Coolangatta"	1	1	0
Beilby, E. T.	2	2	0
Butterworth, H., Bathurst	2	2	0
Betts, Miss, Glebe Point Road	2	2	0
Bransby, C. S., Moss Vale	1	1	0
Biddell Brothers	1	1	0
Bown, C.	1	1	0
Barton, Mrs. Edward, Wallerawang	2	0	0
Bull, W., J.P.	1	0	0
Baillie, Mrs. J. H.	2	2	0

Name	£	s	d
Barker, Rev. H., Sutton Forest	£1	1	0
Broadhurst, Mrs.	1	1	0
Boles, W.	1	1	0
Browu, Andrew, J.P., Lithgow	2	0	0
Brown, S. C., M.P.	2	2	0
Butler, Hon. E., M.L.C....	1	1	0
Bowman, Mrs. W., Richmond	2	0	0
Bowman, Miss, Richmond	1	0	0
Bates, Miss Emma	2	0	0
Brereton, Dr. Le Gay ...	2	2	0
Bright Bros. & Co.	2	2	0
Brown and Co....	1	1	0
Bennett, S.	1	1	0
Blunt, G., Muswellbrook...	2	2	0
Baker, Thomas...	1	1	0
Board, Gregory	2	0	0
Busby, Mrs., Double Bay	2	0	0
Brown, J. A., Newcastle...	1	1	0
Booth, Mrs., Balmain ...	1	1	0
Broillatt, Mrs., Aunandale	1	1	0
Butler, W., Kilcoy, Brisbane	1	1	0
Buzacott and Armstrong	1	1	0
Boltou, Major, Newcastle	1	0	0
Beyers, H. L., M.P., Hill End	1	1	0
Begg, John E.	1	1	0
Bellew, Mrs., Piercefield, Muswellbrook	1	0	0
Briggs, W., West Maitland	2	0	0
Bolding, H. J., Scone ...	1	1	0
Bell, Mrs.	1	1	0
Bird, H. S.	1	1	0
Brush, J.	1	1	0
Blackburn and Co	1	1	0
Black, J. R., J.P. "Wallangra," Warialda ...	1	1	0
Bradley, Newton and Lamb	1	1	0
Bond, C. B.	1	1	0
Brown, Walterns, J.P., Wilcannia	0	10	0
Brown, F., "St. Aubins," Scone	1	0	0
Bryen, S. J.	1	1	0
Bull, Price and Co.	1	1	0
Badgery Brothers, Sutton Forest	1	1	0
Badgery, H., J.P., Vine Lodge, Sutton Forest ...	1	1	0
Badgery, Frederick D., "Hawthorne," Sutton Forest	1	0	0
Conelly, Mrs., Goulburn...	£2	2	0
Capel, D., J.P., Piedmont, Burrah, Collected by ...	1	4	6
Cameron, Alexander, J.P., Rocky Mouth	1	0	0
Carraher, Owen J., J.P....	1	0	0
Campbell, Hon. C., M.L.C.	2	2	0
Cook, Joseph and Co. ...	1	1	0
Cox, Mrs., Goulburn ...	2	0	0
Conolly, T., Seymour ...	0	5	0
Cox, Hon. G. H., Mudgee	2	2	0
Chisholm, A. S.	1	1	0
Campbell, Hon. Alexander, M.L.C., Woollahra ...	2	2	0
Corner, Mrs. J. G.	0	10	0
Caird, Paterson & Co. ...	1	1	0
Cottee, W. A., J.P.... ...	1	1	0
Callaghan and Son	1	1	0
Clare, W.	2	0	0
Crane, W., P.M.	1	1	0
Crane, G. E. & Son	1	1	0
Clapham, R. W., Braidwood	1	1	0
Chauvel, Mrs.	1	0	0
Campbell, A., "Lorn Bank," Macquarie Plains... ...	1	1	0
Cowper, Rev. Dean... ...	1	0	0
Carss, W., Kogerah... ...	1	0	0
Clarke, John	0	5	0
Carmichael, J.	0	5	0
Capper, E. P., and Son, West Maitland	1	1	0
Cameron, Angus, "Angus Villa," North Grafton...	1	0	0
Cox, J. H., "Negoa," Muswellbrook	1	0	0
Clements, J. & B., "Woolbrook," Bigga, Collected by—			
Clements, J. and B. ...	2	0	0
Ridley, E.	1	0	0
Howard, J.	1	0	0
Howard, D.	1	0	0
Nokes, W.	1	0	0
Archer, J.	0	10	0
Spawlding, G.	0	10	0
Fawset, J.	0	5	0
Fraser, A.	0	5	0
Dowdy, T.	0	5	0
Kidley, Miss...	0	2	6
Dandy, O.	0	2	6
Cooper, Nathan and Co....	1	1	0
Cohen, George J., West Maitland	1	1	0

	£	s	d
Campbell, John	0	10	0
Chapman, J. T...	1	1	0
Carmichael, Bros , Seaham	1	0	0
Clarke, Mrs. G. T., Fort st.	1	1	0
Dangar, F. H.	50	0	0
Dight, Mrs Arthur, per Lady Hay	1	0	0
Donald, Rev.W.S.,Clarence Town	1	1	0
Dempsey, G. H., Penrith	0	10	0
Dibbs, T. A., 1877	2	2	0
Dearin, T. B.	1	1	0
Dixson and Sons	1	1	0
Doninthorne, Miss, Newtown	1	1	0
Daintrey, E.	1	1	0
Durham, J., Singleton ...	1	1	0
Davis, R., Brisbane Water	1	1	0
Drummond, James, Bookham	1	0	0
Dunn, Captain, Woodville	1	0	0
Darley, Hon. F., M.L.C....	1	1	0
Dickson, Mrs.," Bolwarra," West Maitland	1	1	0
Dicker, Rev. H., Coonabarabran	1	1	0
Dangar, A. A. " Baroona," Singleton	3	3	0
Durham, G.	2	2	0
Dangar, W.J."Neotsfield," Singleton	2	2	0
Day, W., J.P., " Western Lea," Pyrmont	1	0	0
Docker, Hon. J., M.L.C...	1	1	0
Dight, Mrs. E. M., Singleton...	1	0	0
Dangar, H. C.	3	3	0
Dangar, Mrs. H. C.... ...	1	1	0
Daniel, Mrs. Walcha ...	1	1	0
Doran, Miss	1	1	0
Docker, A. K.	1	0	0
Dibbs, T. A.	2	2	0
DeLissa and Co., 1877 ...	1	1	0
Doyle, J. F. and J. "Kuludah," Lochinvar ...	1	1	0
Day, Mrs. Senr., Pyrmont	1	0	0
Dight, S. B., J.P., donation "Clifford," Singleton ...	1	0	0
Drummond, W., Tenterfield	1	0	0
Dickson, J., Bennett-street, Waverley	2	0	0
E. W. K.	5	0	0
Edols & Co., Thos., Burrawang	2	2	0
Eldridge, W. C.	0	10	6
Elliott, P. J. and Co. ...	1	1	0
Elliott Brothers	1	1	0
Evans, Captain, Newtown	1	1	0
F. J.	1	1	0
Fell, W. C., Braidwood ...	1	1	0
Flower, Miss, 1877	1	1	0
Forsyth, A. and Co	3	3	0
Foster, Teather, T.B., 1877-78	2	2	0
Friend, W. S.	2	2	0
Faithful, W. P., J.P., "Springfield." Goulburn	2	2	0
Frazer, Hon. John, M.L.C.	5	5	0
Frazer, John & Co.	3	3	0
Fawns, Rev. J., Tasmania	1	0	0
Ferguson, G.	1	1	0
Fletcher, J , J.P., Walcha	2	0	0
Farmer and Company ...	1	1	0
Forsyth, G., J.P., " Yarrongabilly," Tumut ...	1	1	0
Finch, H., Newcastle ...	1	1	0
Fache, C. J.	2	2	0
Fairfax, Mrs. C. J.	2	0	0
Freeman,W., "Greenwich," Armidale	1	0	0
Faucett, His Honor Judge	1	1	0
Fairfax, James R.	1	1	0
Fairfax, Edward R.... ...	1	1	0
Flavelle Bros. and Roberts	1	1	0
Fitzpatrick, Hon. M., Colonial Secretary ...	1	0	0
Foley, B.	0	10	6
Friedman, A.	1	1	0
Forsyth, J., and Sons ...	1	1	0
Fortescue, G., M.B. ...	2	2	0
G. J.	2	2	0
Green, James, Surry Hills	1	0	0
Giblin, V. W.	2	2	0
Gray, R., Son, and Co. ...	1	1	0
Gennys, Mrs., Carcoar ...	1	0	0
Griffiths and Co.	2	2	0
Goodlet and Smith	2	2	0
Gilchrist, Watt and Co. ...	1	1	0
Gally, W., Hinton	1	0	0
Gorman, H.	1	1	0
Gibbs, Shallard and Co. ...	2	2	0
Grahame, Hon. W., M.L.C.	1	1	0
Gibson, L. L., Langford, Bendemere	1	0	0

	£	s	d		£	s	d
Gallaway, J., Parramatta	£1	0	0	Horsley, R. F., " Yabtree," Gundagai	£1	1	0
Graham, J., J.P.	1	1	0	Hargrave, E., J.P. " Hernani," Armidale	1	0	0
Gardiner, W., and Co.	2	2	0	Hoskisson, Mrs. J., Windsor	1	0	0
Giblin, T. M.	1	1	0	Hall, Mrs., " Dartbrook," Muswellbrook	1	0	0
Gross, J.C., "Strathbogie," Vegetable Creek	1	1	0	Houison, Mrs., Parramatta	1	1	0
Gill, G. R., J.P., Emu Creek, Walcha	1	1	0	Hurley, John, Glebe	1	1	0
Greenhill, S.	2	2	0	Hawke, G., J.P.. Byng	1	1	0
Gill, J., J.P., Moonby	1	0	0	Horne, S. H., Singleton	1	0	0
Garrick and Co.	1	1	0	Howe, John K., " Redburnbury " Singleton	2	2	0
Gordon, Hon. S. D., M.L.C.	1	1	0	Hooke, Augustus, J.P.,			
Gibson, Frederick F., "Caragubell," Grenfell	1	1	0	" Hamilton Hill," Singleton	1	1	0
Gillman, Dr.	1	1	0	Hamburger, Brothers	2	2	0
Gibbs, Mrs., Ashfield	0	5	0	Holt, Hon. Thomas, M.L.C.	5	0	0
				Hanks, J. G. and Co.	1	1	0
Hookins, C., Albury	1	1	0	Hudson, R , "Warrah," Willow Tree	1	1	0
Hay, Hon. Sir John, M.L.C.	5	0	0	Hoffnung, S., and Co.	1	1	0
Hordern, Lebbius	5	0	0	Harrison, J. S.	1	1	0
Howe, donation	5	0	0	Hills, Robert	1	1	0
Hammond, H. W., Junee	2	0	0	Howell, Mrs. P.	1	1	0
Hammond, T. W., Junee	1	0	0	Harris, W., Haymarket	1	1	0
Howe, Mrs Anne, Singleton, per Lady Hay	1	0	0	Hough, Rev. W.	0	10	6
Haylock, C. D.	1	1	0	Henry, James, 751 George street	2	2	0
Hassall, Miss	1	0	0	Hardy Brothers, Oxford st.	1	1	0
Hudson Bros.	1	1	0				
Hillier, Mrs.	1	1	0	Iredale, L. F.	2	2	0
Haselton, T.	1	1	0	Isaacs, J. and Co.	2	2	0
Hardy Bros., Hunter street	1	1	0	Isler, Mrs., Petersham	1	0	0
Hobson, Mrs.	1	0	0	Innes, Thomas, Newcastle	1	1	0
Harrison and Attwood	1	1	0				
Hezlet, W., J.P.	0	10	6	Josephson, His Honor Judge, per G. F. Wise	2	2	0.
Hezlet, Mrs.	0	10	6	Jory, Rev. J. D., Fiji, per John Corlett, Esq.	1	0	0
Holdsworth, J. B.	2	2	0	Jones, David and Co.	2	2	0
Hordern, E.	1	1	0	Jones, Dr. P., Sydney	1	1	0
Harrison, Jones & Devlin	3	3	0	Johnston, W., M.P., Clarence Town	1	1	0
Hunt, R.	1	1	0	Jenkins, W. W., J.P., Charcoal	1	0	0
Hargrave, R., " Hill Grove," Armidale	2	0	0	Juye, J., Lawson street, Balmain	1	1	0
Hurley, J., M.P.	1	1	0	Johnson, Rev. Thomas	1	0	0
Harris, John, M.P., Harris street, Ultimo	2	2	0	Jenkins, Dr., J.P., Nepean Towers	5	0	0
Harris, Miss M., Harris street, Ultimo	1	1	0	Jolly, W., J.P., "Essington" Newtown	1	1	0
Hindson, Lawrence	1	1	0	Jay, R. F., Singleton	1	1	0
Humphrey, F. T.	1	1	0				
Hall, T., " Springfield," Waverley	1	1	0				
Hobbs, W. J., Newcastle	1	1	0				
Humphrey, C. H., Burwood	2	2	0				
Hardy, John	1	1	0				
Hall, W. S., J.P.,"Lilburn Hall," Windsor	1	0	0				

	£	s	d		£	s	d
Jones, T. T. and Son ...	£1	1	0	Municipality of Gerringong			
Jones, Stephen...	1	1	0	Collection	£35	2	0
K. B., Port McQuarie,				Myers and Solomon... ...	2	2	0
donation 1877	1	0	0	MacCulloch, T....	1	0	0
Keep, John	1	1	0	Mitchell and Co.	1	1	0
Kent, Mrs., "Elyston,"				Moore, C., J.P....	2	2	0
Woollahra	5	5	0	Moss, Mrs. L. and Sons ...	1	1	0
Keys, J. U., J.P.,				Miller, R....	0	10	6
"Bengalla," Muswell-				Moore, T., Oxford street...	1	1	0
brook	1	1	0	Mitchell, D. S., Darling-			
Kenrick, A, Penrith ...	1	1	0	hurst road	2	0	0
K. B., Port Macquarie ...	1	0	0	Myers and Cantor, 1877...	1	1	0
Kemp, William E.	2	0	0	Mason Brothers	1	1	0
King, Rev. G., M.A.,				Morrisett, E. V., J.P., East			
Burwood	1	0	0	Maitland	1	1	0
Leigh, Mrs., Glen Innes...	0	5	0	Millard, Rev. H. S., New-			
Lassetter, F. and Co. ...	1	1	0	castle	2	0	0
Learmonth, Dickinson & Co.	1	1	0	Moore, E. L., Narellan ...	1	0	0
Lord, E.	1	0	0	Manning, C. J....	2	2	0
Lorimer, Rome and Co. ...	1	1	0	Merewether, Mrs., "The			
Levey, Montague, J.P. ...	1	1	0	Ridge," Newcastle ...	3	3	0
Lester, Miss, Burwood ...	3	3	0	Mitchell, George, Newcastle	1	0	0
Lamb, Mrs.	1	1	0	Marsh, Mrs., "Salisbury			
Leibius, Dr.	1	1	0	Court," Uralla	1	1	0
Leathes, A. Stanger... ...	2	2	0	Maxwell, A. C.	1	1	0
Laidley, W., aud Co. ...	2	2	0	Manning, His Hon. Sir W.	1	1	0
Lamb, Walter, J.P.,				Macintyre, D., Kajugu ...	1	0	0
"Quirang," Edgecliffe				Milne, Rev. J., M.A. ...	1	0	0
road	2	2	0	Moore, J., Singleton ...	1	1	0
Loder, G., "Abbey Green,"				Miller, David, Newcastle	1	1	0
Singleton	2	2	0	Mansfield, G. Allen... ...	1	1	0
Looke, W., Balmain ...	1	0	0	Myers, J. H.	0	10	0
Linsley, J. R., J.P	1	1	0	Moore, W., Elizabeth street	1	0	0
Love, J. R.	1	1	0	Myers and Cantor	1	1	0
Mackellar, Alexander,				Moses, H. M.P., Ashfield	1	1	0
Goulburn 1877	2	2	0	Marks, J., J.P...	5	0	0
Malcolm, Jean, Bequest ...	6	1	8	Mackellar, Dr.	1	1	0
Merriman, J., His Worship				Mackenzie, Dr. W. F. ...	1	1	0
the Mayor	2	2	0	Milson, James, Jun. J.P.,			
Murphy, J. and Son ...	1	0	0	North Shore...	3	3	0
Madgwick, Rev. E. C.,				McIntyre, Rev. D. K., Ti-			
Penrith...	0	10	0	nonce, Manning River...	1	0	0
Maguire, Thomas	5	6	0	McKay, D. F., Singleton	1	0	0
Matthews, donation... ...	0	17	3	MacPherson, P., East			
Martin & Brown	2	2	0	Maitland	1	1	0
Monro, J.	0	10	0	McArthur and Co.	2	2	0
Morehead, R. A. A.... ...	2	2	0	McIntyre, Master, The			
Montefiore, Joseph & Co.	1	1	0	"Manse" Tinonee, Man-			
Mills, John	1	1	0	ning River, Collection—			
Macgregor. J.	1	1	0	Mrs. M'Intyre, 20s ; Wil-			
Macdonnell, W.	0	10	6	liam M'Intyre, 3s. 3d ;			
Metcalfe, Mrs.	1	1	0	Mrs. Hamilton, 5s ; J.			
Maxwell, A. H.	1	1	0	D. St. Clair M'Lardy, 5s;			
				Mrs. Leefe, 5s ; H.			

Evans, 2s. 9d ; H. W. Harding, London, 2s. 6d ; J. Davis, 10s ; H. S. New Zealand, 5s ; Mrs. K. M'Donald, 3s ; S. M'Donald, 2s ; Rev. W. M'Intyre, 20s ; Misses M'Intyre (2), 2s ; W. Thompson, 2s ; R. Frame, 2s ; Samuel Stewart, 5s ; J. W. Mann, 2s 6d ; E. Burdett, 2s. 6d ; Friend, 2s 6d ; J. Belford, 2s 6d ; D. M'Donald, 2s 6d ; E. Boyce, 2s 6d ; William Featherstone, 2s 6d ; J. M. D. 2s. 6d ; Mary Trotter, 2s 6d ; A. M'Kay, 2s ; Mary M'Kay, 5s ; John M'Kay, 2s ; Angus M'Kay, 2s 6d ; Ida B. Slott, 2s 6d ; Mary Ann Slott, 2s 6d ; A. M'Leod, 3s ; Thomas Frost, 5s ; Mrs. Wichard, 1s ; Mina 1s ; A. R. H., 2s 6d ; Mrs. M'Donald, 1s ; Mrs. Beattie, 5s ; Mrs. M'Leuine, 5s ; W. Bentsman, 2s 6d ; J. Wallis, 1s ; J. Bowes, 5s ; E. A. M., 2s 6d ; D. McLennon, 2s 6d ; Friend, 1s ; Mrs. Wotten, 1s ; J. Robinson, 1s ; J. Peiry, 1s ; A. Francis, 1s ; J. Melthen, 1s ; G. Saxby, 1s ; S. Plummer, 1s ; A. Cameron, 2s ; N. Mc Lean, 2s 6d ; J. McLean, 2s 6d ; friend, 2s 6d ; Belford, 2s 6d ; S. Whitbread, 2s ; R. W. Orton, 5s ; friend, 2s 6d ; M. McLennon, 2s ; R. J. Wall, 2s ; J. A. Churchill, 2s. 6d ; E. Wynter, 2s 6d ; Mrs. McKenna, 2s 6d ; J. Dennis, 2s ; Mrs. Ball, 1s ; Mrs. Avery, 2s 6d ; J. B. Caris, 2s 6d ; A.

	£	s	d
Simpson, 2s ; A. Hawkins, 2s 6d ; Adam Stokes, 5s ; Mrs. J. Keats, 3s ; friend, 1s ; W. Dawson, 2s 6d ; J. M. P. Ainsworth, 2s 6d ; John Murray, 2s 6d ; Eliza Wilkes, 2s 6d ; Wm. Dawson, 1s 6d ; John Kennedy, 2s 6d ; Mrs. Windsor, 2s ; Mrs. Powell, 2s ; A. E. Else, 2s ; Mrs. Galloway, 2s ; W. Armstrong, 2s ; Mrs. McMin, 2s 6d ; Anon, 1s ;	12	17	0
McDouall, J. C. J.P., "New Frugh" Singleton	0	10	6
McDonald, Smith and Co.	1	0	0
N. P. C.	5	0	0
Norton, A. C.	2	2	0
Noake, J.	0	10	0
Newton C., Bros., and Co.	2	2	0
Nichol, D....	1	0	0
Norton, James	1	1	0
Newman, J. Hubert... ...	1	1	0
O'Neil, Michael	1	0	0
Osborne, Miss, per F. P. McCabe, J.P., Wollongong	5	0	0
Oriental Bank	5	5	0
Old, R., North Shore ...	2	0	0
O'Reilly, Rev. Canon ...	1	0	0
Pettit, Mrs., Crown street	2	2	0
Peate and Harcourt... ...	2	2	0
Prince, Ogg and Co. ...	2	2	0
Perry, W., and Company	1	1	0
Poolman, S.	1	1	0
Pemell, J...	1	1	0
Paige, J. F.	1	1	0
Plummer, James	1	1	0
Perks, F.	1	1	0
Pearson, S. J., Parramatta	2	2	0
Perkins, Mr. Thomas, Balmain	1	0	0
Perdriau, H., J.P.	1	1	0
Palser, H. P., J.P.	0	10	0
Parbury, C.	1	1	0
Perrett, J., "Tyringham," South Grafton	1	0	0
Phillips, F.	1	1	0
Peberdy, Thomas, Mayor, Tenterfield	1	1	0

	£	s	d
Peapes and Shaw	£1	1	0
Potts, Mrs. J. H., North Shore	3	0	0
Phillips, H.	1	1	0
Peck, Isaac	2	2	0
Quinn, William, legacy...	25	0	0
Queens Masonic Lodge, Penrith, 982 E. C. W.M. Bro. John Tipping ...	2	10	0
Robinson, Mrs. G. L., Windsor, 1877	1	0	0
Robinson and Greenwell, Windsor	1	0	0
Rutherford, J., J.P., Bathurst	1	1	0
Raphael, J. G., J.P. ...	1	1	0
Robison, Hugh...	1	0	0
Robinson, Mrs. G. L., "The Grange," Windsor ...	1	0	0
Ryrie, J. C., "Weambah," Dubbo	1	1	0
Russell, H. C., B.A. ...	1	1	0
Russell, P. N.	1	1	0
Ralston, A. J.	1	1	0
Ross, J. Grafton	1	1	0
Ross Morgan and Co. ...	1	1	0
Renwick, G.J.P. (1877-78)	2	2	0
Reeve, T. P.	1	0	0
Roberts, C. J.	1	1	0
Roseby, J., M.P.	0	10	0
Richardson and Wrench...	2	2	0
Roberts, Mrs. Mary... ...	7	7	0
Ryan, E. J.P., Grafton ...	1	1	0
Richards, B. Windsor ...	1	1	0
Rankin, A. H., J.P., Goulburn	1	1	0
Rourke, J., West Maitland	1	1	0
Reading, Mrs. E.	1	1	0
Rotton, H., J.P., "Blackdown," Bathurst... ...	1	1	0
Rush, Sub Inspector ...	1	0	0
Renwick, Dr.	2	2	0
Ryrie, S., "Cavan," Yass	1	0	0
Ross, G. and Co.	2	2	0
Rabone, Feez and Co. ...	1	1	0
Robinson, His Excellency Sir Hercules, K.C.B. &c.	3	0	0
Robinson, F. R.	1	1	0
Robertson, T.	1	1	0
St. Stephen's Presbyterian Church, per Alexander Dean	2	0	0
Small, Timothy, Ryde, Jurors fees, donation ...	£0	19	4
Scott, Rev. W....	1	0	0
Star of Macleay Masonic lodge, No. 600 S. C. ...	1	1	0
St. John's Lodge, I. O. O. F. M. U. Donation per H. Howe	10	10	0
Samaritan collected in, boxes	5	1	8
Smith, Ernest O.	1	1	0
Staff, Mrs. J. F.	1	0	0
Suttor, Hon. W. H., Bathurst, donation ...	10	0	0
Smith, John, J.P.,"Llanark," Bathurst	1	1	0
Simpson, G.	1	1	0
Sly, J.	1	1	0
Samuel, Hon. Saul, C.M.G., M.L.C.	1	1	0
Smyth, S. H.	2	2	0
Smart, Hon. T. W., M.L.C., "Mona"	2	2	0
Slade, G. P.	1	1	0
Sparke, W. E.	1	1	0
Smith and Mannell	1	1	0
Schuette, Dr. R.	1	1	0
Sydney, Lord Bishop of ...	2	2	0
Smyth and Wells	0	10	0
Scott, D.	1	1	0
Scott, Walter, J.P. "Wallalong," Hinton	1	0	0
Stephen, M. H.	3	0	0
Saunders, J. M., West Maitland	1	1	0
Stedman, J.	1	1	0
Stewart, Rev. Colin	1	0	0
Smith, Rev. Pierce Galliard, Canberra	1	1	0
Saber, W. and Sons ...	2	2	0
Speer, W., J.P. 1877 ...	1	1	0
Spring, J.	1	1	0
Smith, Hawkins	1	1	0
Strickland, J., "Bunderburra," Forbes	1	1	0
Smith, Hon. Dr. M.L.C.	1	1	0
Simpson, W. H.	1	1	0
Sun Kum On	0	10	0
Skarratt, C. C. J.P.... ...	1	1	0
Street, J. R.	1	1	0
Starkey, J.	1	1	0
Sloper, F. E.	1	1	0
Shadler, A.	1	1	0
Speer, W. J.P....	1	1	0

Name	£	s	d
Scott, Mrs., Surveyors Creek, Walcha	£1	0	0
Saul, Washington H. ...	1	1	0
Suit in District Court per Wainman	0	12	6
Smith, Shepherd, N. S. Wales Bank, don... ...	10	0	0
Smith, Shepherd	2	2	0
Statham, E. J., Grafton ...	2	2	0
Stephen, Sir Alfred C.B., K.C.M.G.	1	1	0
Todhunter, H. M., Mudgee donation	20	0	0
Town, A. R., Richmond ...	1	1	0
Taylor, H. J.	1	0	0
Thatcher, Mrs. J. Cavan, per Rev. W. H. H. Yarrington	1	0	0
Thomas,Henry A.,"Wivenhoe," Narellan	2	2	0
Tucker and Co.	1	1	0
Thompson, R.	0	10	6
Tooth and Co.	2	2	0
Thompson and Giles ...	2	2	0
Tucker, W., J.P.	1	1	0
Towns, R. and Co.	1	1	0
Trebeck, Mr. and Mrs. ...	1	1	0
Thorne, Mrs. R.	2	2	0
Thompson, A., J.P.	1	1	0
Threlkeld, L. E. and Co....	2	2	0
Thornton, Hon. G., M.L.C.	1	1	0
Thomson, Sir E. Deas, C.B., K.C.M.G.	1	1	0
Threlkeld, Mrs., Burwood	1	1	0
Talbot and Son...	2	2	0
Thompson, R. W., West Maitland	1	1	0
Tranter, R., Albion Farm, West Maitland	0	10	6
Throsby, P. H., Moss Vale	1	1	0
Trickett, W. J....	1	1	0
Uzzell, Rev. W. F. B., Balmain	0	10	6
Visitors' box at Institution	8	18	3
Ditto after Annual Meeting	3	0	0
Vickery, E.	£2	0	0
Voss, Houlton H., J.P. ...	2	2	0
Verey, S. H. and G., Balmain	1	1	0
Walker, Thomas, Concord	10	0	0
Walker, Miss, ditto... ...	5	0	0
Wade, John, Dungog ...	1	1	0
Woolnough and Co... ...	1	1	0
Wearing, B. C...	1	1	0
Way, E.	1	1	0
Woolcott, W. P.	1	1	0
Watson, John	1	1	0
Wilshire, F. R., P.M., Berrima...	1	1	0
Woodward,F.,Wollongong	1	1	0
White, Hon. James,"Cranbrook," Rose Bay ...	2	0	0
Watkins, F. T...	1	1	0
Want and Johnson	1	1	0
Wolfe and Gorrick, West Maitland	1	1	0
White, Rev. Canon, Muswellbrook	1	1	0
Wood Brothers, Newcastle	1	1	0
Wright, P. M., J.P., "Bickham,"Murrurundi	1	1	0
White, Mrs. F., Muswellbrook	1	0	0
Windeyer, J., J.P., "Kinross," Raymond Terrace	3	3	0
Wallace, George,Newcastle	1	1	0
Wingate, Mrs.	1	1	0
Williams, John	1	1	0
Wise, George F.	1	1	0
Wilkinson, His Hon. Justice	2	0	0
White, Frederick R., J.P., "Harben Vale," Blanford	2	0	0
Young, James, South Creek	2	5	0
Yeates, W. G.	1	1	0
Young and Lark	1	1	0
Zions, H.	1	1	0

☞ To Subscribers or Friends in the country districts who desire to help the Institution by collecting on behalf of the Funds, Subscription Lists or Cards will be forwarded on application to the Hon. Treasurer or Hon. Secretary—and the amounts received thankfully acknowledged.

Country Collections,
PER MR. GEORGE LUFF.

NEW SOUTH WALES.

Various Towns are placed in alphabetical order.

Donations under 5s. are placed in Lump Sums.

ADELONG.

	£	s.	d.
Budd, W.	1	1	0
Williams, Mrs. E.	1	0	0
Wilson, D., J.P.	1	0	0
Ritchie, W.	1	0	0
White, Rev. W. M.	1	0	0
Broughton, Mrs.,"Gadara"	1	0	0
Fry, J. W.	0	10	6
Richardson, J.	0	10	6
Shaw, Mrs.	0	10	6
Curtis, Mrs.	0	10	0
Kennedy, Dr.	0	10	0
Garland, W. J.	0	10	0
Ball, J., " Mingay "	0	10	0
Williams, W. Jun.	0	10	0
Eagan, R.	0	10	0
Beegling, W.	0	10	0
Griot, L.	0	10	0
Smith, A.	0	10	0
Hodgson, J.	0	10	0
Munlove, W.	0	10	0
Lawson, J.	0	5	6
Tillett, Mrs.	0	5	0
Williams, W., Sen.	0	5	0
Dean, A.	0	5	0
Lee, M.	0	5	0
Deighton, J.	0	5	0
Deighton, W.	0	5	0
Wells, Mrs.	0	5	0
Walker, D.	0	5	0
Boston, D.	0	5	0
Kenny, P.	0	5	0
Byrnes, P.	£0	5	0
Matthews, R.	0	5	0
Youngman, Rev. H.	0	5	0
Latham, H. B.	0	5	0
Eyles, E.	0	5	0
Thomas, R. F.	0	5	0
Thomas, W. G.	0	5	0
Farrington, H.	0	5	0
Lang, Miss	0	5	0
Cowan, M.	0	5	0
Bray, A.	0	5	0
Hotten, W.	0	5	0
Passlow, C.	0	5	0
White, W., Lower Tareutta	0	5	0
Sums under 5s.	0	10	0

APPIN.

Labatt, R. H.	1	0	0
Byrne, J.	0	5	0
Sums under 5s.	0	5	0

BEGA.

Walker, H.	1	1	0
Haslingden, G.	1	1	0
Hand, F.	1	0	0
Peden, M. J., J.P.	1	0	0
Gowing, D., "Jellat Jellat"	1	0	0
Thomson and French	1	0	0
Garrard, C. A.	1	0	0
Faunce, Rev. A. D.	0	10	6
Shiels, Dr.	0	10	6
Evershed, Dr.	0	10	6
Jauncey, J., J.P.	0	10	6

Name	£	s.	d.
Davis, J., P.M.	0	10	6
Connelly, J.	0	10	6
Allen, W., "Warragabra"	0	10	6
Waddell, Rev. J.	0	10	0
Wood, P. H.	0	10	0
Maher, J. M.	0	10	0
Enley, W. R.	0	10	0
Haslingden, J. E.	0	10	0
Rixon and Co.	0	10	0
Welby, O.	0	10	0
Brown, S.	0	5	0
Otton, H.	0	5	0
Wilson, H.	0	5	0
Brown, H.	0	5	0
Jones, T. R.	0	5	0
Thompson, F. C.	0	5	0
Wright, G. A.	0	5	0
Kennedy, M.	0	5	0
H. P.	0	5	0
Wilson, W. H.	0	5	0
A Friend	0	5	0
Magner, T.	0	5	0
Williams, T.	0	5	0
Underhill, H.	0	5	0
Harrison, C.	0	5	0
Witton, Mrs.	0	5	0
Sums under 5s	0	7	6
Bega Standard Advertisements free			
Fowler, H., "Wolumba"	0	7	6
Morehead, W. J., ditto	0	5	0

BIBBENLUKE.

Name	£	s.	d.
Rutherford, Mrs., "Minto"	2	0	0
Campbell, Mrs.	1	1	0
Edwards, H. T., J.P.	1	0	0
Horne, W. J.	0	5	0
Piesley, C.	0	5	0

BODALLA.

Name	£	s.	d.
Mort, T. S., 1877-78	4	4	0
Hoyle, Mrs.	0	5	0
Bryan, E.	0	5	0

BOMBALA.

Name	£	s.	d.
Whyte, Henry P.	1	0	0
Myers, David M.	1	1	0
Reeve, Rev. G. A.	1	1	0
Joseph, H. M., J.P., "Maharatta"	1	1	0
Bundock, W. F.	1	1	0
Cooke, W. V. M., J.P.	1	0	0
Cruckshank, J., J.P.	1	0	0
Hatton, Mrs. and Miss B.	0	13	0
Hayes, H., J.P.	0	10	6
Stevenson, J.A., J.P. "Mila"	0	10	6
Lightbody, T. R.	0	10	6
Thorne, T. W.	0	10	0
Hill, S.	0	10	0
Lipscomb, B.	0	10	0
Betts, Rev. J. C.	0	10	0
Langhorn, J.	0	10	0
Oberthur, J. E.	0	5	0
Badgery, Mrs.	0	5	0
Burgess, Mrs.	0	5	0
Bennett, John E., J.P.	0	5	0
Hogarth, H.	0	5	0
A Friend	0	5	0
Hyde, E.	0	5	0
Lamb, Mrs.	0	5	0
Robinson, J. D.	0	5	0
Dent, Mrs.	0	5	0
Hardaker, W.	0	5	0
King, G.	0	5	0
Jonas, E.	0	5	0
Tweedie, C. L.	0	5	0
Giles, J., J.P., C.P.S.	0	5	0
Sums under 5s	0	12	6
Ditto per favor of Giles, J.	0	10	0
Bombala Herald, Advertisements free			

BRAIDWOOD.

Name	£	s.	d.
Bryce, Rev. J. G.	1	1	0
Maddrell, R. J. C., "Mona Cottage"	1	1	0
Llewellyn, Dr. Kees, J.P.	1	1	0
Payne and Sandford	1	1	0
Musgrave, J., *Braidwood Dispatch*	1	1	0
Fell, W. C.	1	1	0
Clapham, R. W.	1	1	0
Maddrell, R., J.P., "Bedervale"	1	0	0
Coghill, Mrs., ditto	1	0	0
Roberts, T. J., "Exeter Farm"	1	0	0
Tweedie, G.	1	0	0
Robertson, W. F., C.P.S.	0	10	6
Robinson, C. C.	0	10	6
Wallace, J., J.P., "Nithsdale"	0	10	6
Steward, T., J.P.	0	10	6
Kingsland, J.	0	10	6
Darke, W.	0	10	0
Fraser, J.	0	10	0
Wilson, H. P.	0	10	0
Roberts, C. H.	0	10	0

Royds, W. E.	£0	10	0
Philpotts, H. J	0	10	0
Hicks, D. S.	0	10	0
Kartzmann, C.	0	10	0
Dillon, J. M.	0	5	0
Ball, W.	0	5	0
A Friend	0	5	0
McKellor, J, ...	0	5	0
McDowell, W.	0	5	0
A Friend	0	5	0
Bruce, R.	0	5	0
Hyland, P...	0	5	0
Williams, J. V., "Boro"	0	5	0
Sums under 5s....	0	6	0

BROUGHTON CREEK.

Boyd, Adam, J.P.	1	0	0
Wilson, J. and Co.	0	10	0
Elkin, Rev. J.	0	10	0
Beaumont, G.	0	5	0
Tate, G.	0	5	0
Warren, R. H.	0	5	0
Donaldson, H. T.	0	5	0
Boyd, Mrs.	0	5	0

BROGO.

Brown, C.	1	0	0
McGregor, J.	0	2	6

BULLI.

Ross, Alexander, J.P. ...	0	10	0
Smith, E. M.	0	10	0
Wollas, H....	0	5	0
Turnbull, G.	0	5	0
Artis, A. S.	0	5	0
Sums under 5s....	0	8	0
Fry, H., J.P., "Woonona"	0	5	0

BUNGENDORE.

Powell, W. G., J.P., "Taratta"	1	1	0
McJannett, J.	1	1	0
Dodwell, Rev. J. C.... ...	0	10	6
Burke, J. B., J.P.	0	10	0
McClung, A.	0	5	0
Laws, E. K.	0	5	0
Leahy, D....	0	5	0
Marsden, Mrs....	0	5	0
Ross, C.	0	5	0
Johnson, W.	0	5	0
Noonan, J.	0	5	0
McMahon, J.	0	5	0
Sums under 5s....	0	16	0

BURROWA.

Hume, F. R., Sen., J.P. "Castlestead"	£2	2	0
Hume, A. Hamilton, J.P. Donation, "Everton"...	2	2	0
Gwynne, Rev. Canon ...	1	1	0
Scott, H. P., J.P.	1	1	0
Pett, W. B.	1	1	0
Campbell, W. D., J.P. ...	1	1	0
Ryan, J. N., J.P.	1	1	0
Cummins, T.	1	0	0
Kenane, D. R.	0	10	6
Hume, Mrs. F. W.	0	10	6
Hume, F. W.	0	10	6
Hayes, Mrs.	0	10	0
Wotton, W. J. E., J.P., C.P.S.	0	10	0
Stevenson, J.	0	10	0
A Friend	0	10	0
Worms, L. H.	0	5	0
Hitch, N. B.	0	5	0
O'Rourke, Mrs. J. B. ...	0	5	0
Mackey, G. G....	0	5	0
Gardiner, T. S....	0	5	0
Allsopp, T.	0	5	0
Russell, C. W.	0	5	0
James, T. L.	0	5	0
J. K....	0	5	0
O'L., F. J.	0	5	0
Sums under 5s....	0	11	0

CAMBEWARRA.

Richards, Mrs. T. Morton	1	1	0
Matthews, S.	0	10	0
Fraser, J., J.P....	0	7	6
Brice, Z. G., J.P.	0	5	0
Hyndes, E.	0	5	0
Shepherd, T.	0	5	0
Montgomery, H.	0	5	0
McKenzie, K.	0	5	0
McGrath, W.	0	5	0
Gibson, J....	0	5	0
Sums under 5s...	0	6	6

CAMPBELLTOWN.

Aikin, Rev. T. V., M.A....	1	1	0
Hurley, J., M.P.	1	1	0
Suttor, F. W., J.P., "Varroville"...	1	1	0
Reddall, Misses, "Glen Alpine"	1	1	0
Woodhouse, J. B., J.P., "Mount Gilead" ...	1	1	0

	£	s	d
Blomfield, R. H., J.P., "Denham Court"	1	0	0
Fowler, W., J.P.	1	0	0
Kidd, J., J.P.	0	10	0
Fowler, D.	0	10	0
Scouler, Mrs.	0	5	0
Booking. J.	0	5	0
Brown, G.	0	5	0
Stewart, T.	0	5	0
Mackel, F.	0	5	0
Warby, J.	0	5	0
Payton, J.	0	5	0
Warby, B.	0	5	0
Dwyer, P.	0	5	0
Humphries, J. P.	0	5	0
Sums under 5s	1	1	6

CANDELO.

	£	s	d
A Friend	0	10	6
Smith, P. E.	0	10	0
Hammond, H.	0	10	0
Cochrane, J.	0	10	0
Collins, J.	0	5	0
Draper, G.	0	5	0
Sharpe, J. W.	0	5	0
Ramsey, J.	0	5	0
Meures, E.	0	5	0
Tapper, T.	0	5	0
Sums under 5s	0	6	0

CATHCART.

	£	s	d
Kesterton, W.	1	0	0
Horsey, Mrs.	0	5	0
Sullivan, Mrs.	0	5	0
Brown, Miss	0	5	0
Gerathy, Mrs.	0	5	0
Taylor, C.	0	5	0
Sums under 5s	0	2	0

COBARGO.

	£	s	d
Stennett, T., J.P.	0	10	6
Tarlington, W. D., "Bredbatoura"	0	10	0
Roberts, Mrs.	0	5	0
O'Reilly, J.	0	5	0

CHARCOAL.

	£	s	d
Jenkins, W. W., J.P.	1	1	0
Richards, J., Mayor	0	10	0
Lindsay, J., J.P.	0	5	0
Beaties, P.	0	5	0

COOMA.

	£	s	d
Boucher, J.	1	1	0
Betts, A. C.	1	1	0
Bloomfield, A., J.P., "Marinambla"	1	1	0
Pratt, S. A., J.P., "Myalla"	1	1	0
Solomon, C.	1	1	0
Cohen, G., Cooma Hotel	1	1	0
Spring, G. W., *Munro Mercury*	1	1	0
Cosgrove, J., J.P., "Billybingra"	1	1	0
Dawson, R., P.M.	1	0	0
Battye, Captain, J.P.	1	0	0
McGeorge, J.	1	0	0
Scott, J.	1	0	0
Mawson, J. J.	1	0	0
Hain, S.	0	12	0
Druitt, Rev. Canon	0	10	6
Smithers, G. S., C.P.S.	0	10	6
Beazley, J. G.	0	10	6
Lazarus, D.	0	10	6
Fisher, G. L.	0	10	6
Crang, W. B.	0	10	6
Hands, J.	0	10	0
Hain, J., Sen.	0	10	0
Margoschis, E.	0	10	0
Carey, W. B.	0	10	0
Gale, A.	0	10	0
Thornton, H.	0	10	0
Hain, Joseph	0	10	0
Stewart, H.	0	10	0
Kirwan, J.	0	10	0
Wild, J.	0	10	0
Birch, K.	0	10	0
O'Rourke, D.	0	10	0
Cullen, J.	0	10	0
McCarthy, Mrs.	0	7	6
Brennan, C. J.	0	5	0
Bailey, G.	0	5	0
Hain, Mrs. Emma	0	5	0
Poidevin, P.	0	5	0
Lucy, M.	0	5	0
Warne, G.	0	5	0
Davis, T.	0	5	0
Walker, J.	0	5	0
Curtis. A.	0	5	0
F. P. B.	0	5	0
Dodds, E.	0	5	0
Sums under 5s	0	4	6

COOTAMUNDRA.

	£	s	d
O'Donnell, P. J., J.P.	1	0	0
Hurley, J. B.	1	0	0
Barnes, J. and E.	1	0	0
Kirby, J.	0	10	0

	£	s	d
Jones, R.	£0	10	0
Simpson, J.	0	10	0
Webster, T. J....	0	10	0
Cootamundra Herald ...	0	10	0
Strongitharm, E.	0	10	0
Powell, P., "Wallenbeen"	0	10	0
Taylor, A. N.	0	5	0
Crabbe, Dr.	0	5	0
Primrose, C. H. B.	0	5	0
Matthews Brothers	0	5	0
Noble, J.	0	5	0
Mackenzie and Archer ...	0	5	0
Mooney, E. C.	0	5	0
McBeath, T.	0	5	0
Purcell, Mrs.	0	5	0
McCullock, J.	0	5	0
Sums under 5s....	0	14	6
Cootamundra Herald, Advertisements free			

DAPTO.

	£	s	d
Griffin, J. F.	0	5	0
Phillips, Mrs.	0	5	0
McRae, D.	0	5	0
Hewitt, W.	0	5	0
Baylis, Joseph G.	0	5	0
Moffatt, J.	0	5	0

DELEGATE.

	£	s	d
Nicholson, J., "Glen View Grange"	1	0	0
Nicholson, Mrs., ditto ...	0	10	0
Nicholson, Miss, ditto ...	0	5	0
Young Friends, ditto ...	0	12	0
Lawson, J. J., "Craigie"	1	0	0
Haydon, H.	1	0	0
McKeachie, A....	1	0	0
Sellers, W.	0	5	0

DUBBO.

	£	s	d
Sullivan, P., "Cowga" ...	2	0	0
Orbell, W. G.	1	5	0
McDiarmid, N. K.	1	1	0
Stevens and Co.	1	1	0
Coen and Dunn	1	1	0
Egan, J. F., "Mount Harris"...	1	1	0
Heatou, E...	1	1	0
Ryrie, J. C., J.P., "Weambah"	1	1	0
McKillop, Messrs., "Terra Bella"	1	0	0
Samuels, J., Jun., J.P. ...	1	0	0
Yeo, J.	1	0	0

	£	s	d
Friends	£1	0	0
Chapman, W. R., "Mullah"	1	0	0
Fitzgerald, C. H.	0	10	6
Holmes, J.	0	10	6
Fitzhardinge, C. H.... ...	0	10	6
Rabone, Rev. W. T... ...	0	10	6
Wright, Rev. E. H.... ...	0	10	6
Ryan, R. J. J....	0	10	6
Caro, J.	0	10	6
Roxborough, H.	0	10	0
Clouting, J. R....	0	10	0
Tibbits, Dr. J. P.	0	10	0
Tinlay Brothers	0	10	0
Moffatt, W.	0	10	0
Irving, D. M., "Barndilla"	0	10	0
Heane, E. R., "Barbigal"	0	10	0
Gillis, D. M., "Murrundundy"...	0	10	0
Norton, J. O., P.M.... ...	0	2	0
Taylor, G. H., J.P., Mayor	0	5	0
Rourke, S....	0	5	0
Parker, S....	0	5	0
Samuels, A. C....	0	5	0
Benton, A.	0	5	0
Giugni, C....	0	5	0
Olver, W. R.	0	5	0
Blacket, E. N.	0	5	0
Links, G.	0	5	0
Peters, J.	0	5	0
Raper, W. P.	0	5	0
Granger, E.	0	5	0
Yeo, J. E....	0	5	0
Tuck, W. H.	0	5	0
West, J.	0	5	0
Carr, J.	0	5	0
Farney, T...	0	5	0
Muller, N....	0	5	0
Moore, J.	0	5	0
Bertram, A.	0	5	0
Smith, F., J.P....	0	5	0
Booth, R.	0	5	0
Mitchell, R.	0	5	0
Irwin, J. T.	0	5	0
Sums under 5s....	0	5	0
Dubbo Dispatch Advertisements free			

EDEN.

	£	s	d
Russell, Captain B.	2	0	0
Shultz, J. A.	1	0	0
Solomon, S. and H., J.P...	0	10	6
Keon, J., P.M....	0	10	6
Hays, R. B., C.P.S.... ...	0	10	6
Kebby, C....	0	10	6
Barclay, Mrs.	0	6	0

EUROBODALLA.

Coman, W.	... ...	£0	10	0
Brice, C. ...	... ...	0	5	0
Harper, H.	... ...	0	3	0

FORBES.

Thomas, J. and W. ...	...	1	1	0
Fraser, J., J.P. ...	...	1	1	0
Manson, J. and Co. ...	...	1	1	0
Bodel, J., Mayor	... ...	1	1	0
St. Baker and Harwood	...	1	1	0
Fisher, John, Condobolin		1	1	0
Stokes, A., J.P.	... ...	1	1	0
Moore, Brothers, and Co...		1	1	0
Coonan and Dunn	... ...	1	1	0
Nicholas and Raymond	...	0	10	6
Dalton, F. ...	... ...	0	10	6
Morrow, F.	... ...	0	10	6
Elder, H. ...	... ...	0	10	6
Loder, T. J.	... .	0	10	6
Croft, R. ...	... ...	0	10	6
Whelan, E. B. ...	... ...	0	10	6
Dunstan, Rev. E.	... ...	0	10	6
Wood, J. ...	... ...	0	10	0
Z. S. ...	... ...	0	10	0
Brigstock, C. ...	... ...	0	10	0
Cabot, C. ...	... ...	0	5	0
Davies, J. C.	... ...	0	5	0
George, A. S.	... ...	0	5	0
Jones, W. ...	... ...	0	5	0
Smith, W. O. ...	... ...	0	5	0
Bray, E. ...	... ...	0	5	0
Hand, F. ... · ...	... ...	0	5	0
McMillan Brothers ...	...	0	5	0
Bollinger, G. ...	... ...	0	5	0
Hutchinson, G.	... ...	0	5	0
Mitchell, J.	... ...	0	5	0
J. W. ...	... ...	0	5	0
Clancy, H...	... ...	0	5	0
Sums under 5s. ...	... ...	0	7	0

Forbes Times, Advertisements free ... ...
Forbes Gazette, Advertisements free ... ...

GEJEZERICK.

Brooks, A,, J.P.	... ...	1	1	0
Hopburn, W. R.	... ...	1	1	0
Oliver, W.	... ...	0	10	0
Evans, R., Kiah Lake	...	0	5	0

GERRINGONG.

Gray, S. W., M.P. ...	...	1	1	0
Wilson, Rev. Robert	...	1	0	0

Miller, W. ...	... ...	... £0	10	0
Hindmarsh, W., J.P.	...	0	10	0
McNab, W.	... ...	0	10	0
Miller, R., J.P., Mayor	...	0	5	0
Davis, G. F. ...	... ...	0	5	0
Hindmarsh, G. ...	... ...	0	5	0
Sums under 5s. ...	... ...	0	5	0

GININDERRA.

Harcourt, G. ...	... ...	1	0	0
McCarthy, W. R., J.P., "Charnwood"	... ...	0	10	0
Donnelly, P. J. B., "Bywing," Gundaroo...	...	0	10	0

GOULBURN.

Faithfull, W. P., J.P., "Springfield"	... ...	2	2	0
Conelly, Mrs. ...	... ...	2	2	0
Mackellar, Alexander, J.P.		2	2	0
Finley, A. G., J.P. ...	...	2	2	0
Bartlett and Oddy ...	...	2	2	0
Cox, Mrs. ...	... ...	2	0	0
Right Rev. Lord Bishop of Goulburn	... ...	1	1	0
Zouch, Captain, J.P.	...	1	1	0
Conolly, W., J.P. ...	...	1	1	0
Puddicombe, The Ven. Archdeacon		1	1	0
Gibson, Andrew, J.P., "Turanna"		1	1	0
Alexander, C. S.,J.P.,C.P.S.		1	1	0
Chisholm, J. W., J.P., "Wollogorang"		1	1	0
Ranken, W. B., J.P., "Lockyersleigh"		1	1	0
Davidson, Dr., J.P. ...	...	1	1	0
DeLauret, A. G., J.P., "Wynella"		1	1	0
Ball, E., Mayor	... ...	1	1	0
Banks, E. ...	... ...	1	1	0
Dudley, F. H. Pegus	...	1	1	0
Gannon, J. T. ...	... ...	1	1	0
Joplin, R. C.	... ...	1	1	0
Allen, J. T.	... ...	1	1	0
Twynam, E.	... ...	1	1	0
Betts, A. M.	... ...	1	1	0
Caldwell, J.	... ...	1	1	0
Gentle, Dr., J.P.	... ...	1	1	0
Rankin, A. H.,J.P., "Lockyersleigh"		1	1	0
Ross, Mrs.	... ...	1	0	0
Dignam, P.	... ...	1	0	0
Hayes, J. S., J.P.	... ...	1	0	0

	£	s	d
Shepherd, I.	£1	0	0
Riley, W. R.	1	0	0
Lane, W.	1	0	0
Chisholm, W., J.P., "Merrilla"	1	0	0
Hayley, W. F., J.P... ...	0	10	6
Jessop, J. ...	0	10	6
Butler and Co.... ...	0	10	6
Craig, R.	0	10	6
Wood and Co. ...	0	10	6
Warren, Dr.	0	10	6
Foxall, W. S.	0	10	6
Brownhill, J.	0	10	0
Allman, J. J., P.M.... ...	0	10	0
May, Rev. W.	0	10	0
Nash, W. C.	0	10	0
Deacon, F.	0	10	0
Thomas, Mrs. Charles ...	0	10	0
Payten, H.	0	10	0
Slocombe, John ...	0	10	0
Walker, C.	0	10	0
A Friend	0	10	0
O'Brien, J.	0	10	0
Adams, G.	0	10	0
Barber, E. B.	0	10	0
Steer, Mrs.	0	10	0
Fox, J.	0	10	0
Somervile, J.	0	5	0
Davidson, J.	0	5	0
Trenery, J. J.	0	5	0
Lansdowne, A.... ...	0	5	0
Hollis, H.... ...	0	5	0
Simons, J.... ...	0	5	0
Martin, W.	0	5	0
Kerr, A. A.	0	5	0
Hunt, A. M.	0	5	0
Fox, G.	0	5	0
Topham, Mrs.	0	5	0
McAlister, A.	0	5	0
Jacob, T. W.	0	5	0
Gale, W.	0	5	0
Turner, O.... ...	0	5	0
Southall, W.	0	5	0
King, J.	0	5	0
Sums under 5s.... ...	0	2	6
Employees of W. Davies & Co.—			
Davies, W., M.L.A. ...	1	1	0
Channon, J.	0	10	0
Murray, E.	0	10	0
Gardner, C.	0	5	0
Hart, W.	0	5	0
Martin, T.	0	5	0
Mansfield, C... ...	0	2	6
Smith, J.	0	2	6

Southern Argus, Advertisements free ... ...
Evening Penny Post, ditto

GRENFELL.

	£	s	d
Pyne, D., J.P.	£1	1	0
Hill and Halls...	1	1	0
Leeder, W. F.	0	10	6
Mylecharane, W.P., "Cudgelo," Cowra...	0	10	6
Rich, J.	0	10	6
Crommelin, F.	0	10	0
Burgoyne, Dr.	0	10	0
Flannery, G. H.	0	10	0
Nash, H.	0	7	6
Ingery, C. J.	0	5	0
Nowlan, J.	0	5	0
Sums under 5s....	0	12	6

Grenfell Record, Advertisements free ... ...

GUNDAGAI.

	£	s	d
Bootes, Mr. and Mrs., "Mundoro"	1	10	0
Love, W., P.M.	1	1	0
Robinson, J., "Kimo" ...	1	1	0
Smith, W. B., "Darbalara"	1	1	0
Smith, C. H., "Bongongo"	1	1	0
Horsley, R. F., "Yabtree"	1	1	0
Halleron, G. N., J.P. ...	0	10	6
McKillop, Dr.	0	10	6
Walker, M.	0	10	6
Ball, John, "Minchee" ...	0	10	0
Armour, A. W.	0	10	0
Holt, Rev. S. B.	0	10	0
Norton, M.	0	10	0
Smith, Colvile	0	10	0
Allman, E. C.	0	10	0
Mackins, J.	0	10	0
Beveridge, J., Tenandra Park	0	10	0
Leary, J.	0	7	6
Bibo, W.	0	7	6
Engelen, J. B.	0	5	0
O'Sullivan, J.	0	5	0
Shmidt, E.	0	5	0
Passlow, J.	0	5	0
Irving, Mrs.	0	5	0
A Friend	0	5	0
Mackenzie, M. A.	0	5	0
Taylor, S.	0	5	0
Hooworth, J. W. E... ...	0	5	0
Morano, F.	0	5	0
Osmond, W.	0	5	0

Keith, W....	£0	5	0
Sums under 5s....	0	2	6
Gundagai Times, Adver-			
tisements free			

GUNNING.

Taylor, Rev. P. H.	1	1	0
Saxby, H., J.P.	1	0	0
Kenyon, F., J.P., C.P.S....	0	10	6
Jones, A. S., J.P.	0	10	6
Bean, J., Sen.	0	10	0
Busby, W. T.	0	10	0
Grosvener, W....	0	5	0
Conolly, F. W....	0	5	0
Brain, T.	0	5	0
Woodward, R....	0	5	0
Board, P.	0	5	0
Lawliss, F. J.	0	5	0
Sums under 5s....	0	12	0
Advertisements free in			
Gunning Leader			

JAMBEROO.

Marks, S.	0	10	0
Colley, J.	0	10	0
Dymock, D. L....	0	10	0
Stewart, W.	0	5	0
Tate, J.	0	5	0
Tate, J., Jun.	0	5	0
Sums under 5s....	0	5	6

JINDABYNE.

Keon, F., J.P.	0	10	0
Davis, N.	0	10	0
Beattie, W. W...	0	5	0

JUNEE.

Hammond, H. W., J.P....	2	0	0
Hammond, T. W.	1	0	0
Cooney, Owen	1	0	0
Storey, S.	0	10	0
Solomon, M., Bethungra...	0	10	6
Treeweek, J. J., ditto ...	0	5	0

KAMERUKA.

Haslingden, E., J.P., "Coonamata"	1	1	0
Wren, H., J.P.	1	0	0
Stiles, C. F., J.P. and Co., "Kanoona"...	1	0	0
Lane, W. J., J.P.	0	10	0
Champney, T. H.	0	10	0
Bower, Mrs.	0	10	0
Wilkie, R....	0	5	0
Kirby, R. T., J.P., Candelo	0	5	0

KIAMA.

Fuller, G. L., J.P.	£1	1	0
King, W. C.	1	1	0
Pike, Joseph	1	0	0
Davies, W.	0	10	6
Colley, Hugh	0	10	6
Weston, J.	0	10	6
Fuller, T. J.	0	10	0
Hindmarsh, Nesbitt, J.P.	0	10	0
Busby, A....	0	10	0
Black, Major, J.P., Mayor	0	10	0
Reid, S.	0	10	0
Robb, J. S., J.P.	0	10	0
Colley, W.	0	10	0
Kelly, Rev. R. H. D. ...	0	10	0
Kendall, T., J.P.	0	10	0
Finlayson, D.	0	5	0
Mewburn, A. W.	0	5	0
Hunt, G.	0	5	0
Redford, J.	0	5	0
Lewis, W....	0	5	0
Riley, Miss	0	5	0
Colley, J., J.P....	0	5	0
Wood, G....	0	5	0
Fredericks, C.	0	5	0
Tyter, J. F.	0	5	0
Major, S.	0	5	0
Sums under 5s....	0	8	6
Kiama Reporter, Adver-			
tisements free			

MERIMBULA.

Munn's Maizena Company	1	1	0
Morrison, J.	1	1	0
Gibson, A. T.	1	1	0
Smith, R. H.	0	10	0
McPhee, Mrs.	0	10	0
Dennis, G. J.	0	5	0

MICILAGO.

Ryrie, A., J.P....	1	1	0
Cameron Brothers, per W. G. O'Neill	1	0	0
Hayes, M....	0	10	6
Sums under 5s....	0	2	6

MILTON.

Warden, D., J.P., Mayor, "Airlie House"	1	1	0
Ewin, W. W., J.P., "Woodstock"	1	1	0
Allen, J., Jun., "Danes- bank"	1	1	0
Hobbs, T., J.P., "Arenel"	1	1	0

Spooner, Rev. J.	... ...	£1	0 0
Warden, J., J.P.	... ...	1	0 0
Moore, Rev. J....	... ...	0	10 6
Paterson, J.	... ...	0	10 0
Seccombe, R.	... ...	0	10 0
Mathison, Rev. W.	... ...	0	10 0
Miller, J., J.P....	... ...	0	10 0
Kendall, J., J.P.	... ...	0	10 0
Faulks, J., Sen.	... ...	0	6 6
Griffin, W.	... ...	0	5 0
Claydon, H.	... ...	0	5 0
A Friend ...	... ...	0	5 0
Pickering, S.	... ...	0	5 0
McArthur, A.	... ...	0	5 0
Mullan, J....	... ...	0	5 0
Cork, R. ...	... ...	0	5 0
Kendall, T.	... ...	0	5 0
Latta, J. ...	... ...	0	5 0
Kendall, E.	... ...	0	5 0
Millard, H.	... ...	0	5 0
Gruer, W.	... ...	0	5 0
Crommelin, C. E.	... ...	0	5 0
Hayley, W. F....	... ...	0	5 0
Blackburn, H. C.	... ...	0	5 0
Mitchell, T.	... ...	0	5 0
Miller, J. ...	... ...	0	5 0
Watts, D....	... ...	0	5 0
Skillman, H.	... ...	0	5 0
Evans, J. ...	... ...	0	5 0
Hart, Mrs. S.	... ...	0	5 0
Hobbs, F....	... ...	0	5 0
Bong, D. ...	... ...	0	5 0
Brag, A. ...	... ...	0	5 0
Jones, W. G.	.. ...	0	5 0
A Friend ...	... ...	0	5 0
Kendall, W.	... ...	0	5 0
Davies, Miss	... ...	0	5 0
Sums under 5s....	... ...	0	17 6

MOLONG.

Haslam, J.	... ...	1	0 0
Dalrymple, Rev. F. M.	...	0	10 0
Tempest, G. H.	... ...	0	10 0
Hughes, H. M....	... ...	0	10 0
Gardiner, W. A.	... ...	0	10 0
Tanner, W., Jun.	... ...	0	10 0
Ross, Dr. ...	... ...	0	10 0
Phillips, Mrs. ...	... ...	0	10 0
Nisbett, J. H., C.P.S.	...	0	10 0
McGoveron, Mrs.	... ...	0	10 0
Parker, Dr. J. ...	... ...	0	5 0
Parslow, J. T. ...	... ...	0	5 0
Allcroft, R.	... ...	0	5 0
Hicks, H. ...	... ...	0	5 0

Coomber, A.	... ...	£0	5 0
Barlow, E.	... ...	0	5 0
Bowler, J....	... ...	0	5 0
Black, J. ...	... ...	0	5 0
Parker, A....	... ...	0	5 0
Rollo, W. J.	... ...	0	5 0
Gallagher, J. P.	... ...	0	5 0
Mynne, J. F. ...	... ...	0	5 0
Sums under 5s....	... ...	0	9 0

MOLONGLO.

Rutledge, T., J.P., Car- woolo	... ...	1	1 0
Dwyer, T....	... ...	0	10 0
Sums under 5s....	... ...	0	2 6

MORUYA.

Love, Mrs.	... ...	0	10 6
Conolly, R. B. ...	... ...	0	10 6
Caswell, W. S. ...	... ...	0	10 0
Emmatt, A.	... ...	0	10 0
Emmatt, G.	... ...	0	10 0
Allen, H. A.	... ...	0	10 0
Walter, J....	... ...	0	10 0
McKeon, J., J.P.	... ...	0	5 0
Morris, M.	... ...	0	5 0
Shottim, J.	... ...	0	5 0
Aderson, R., J.P.	... ...	0	5 0
Simpson, W. H., J.P.	...	0	5 0
Gannon, T. T., J.P....	...	0	5 0
Clarke, W., C.P.S.	... ...	0	5 0
Collier, W. F.	... ...	0	5 0
Coxou, Mrs.	... ...	0	5 0
Muir, J.	... ...	0	5 0
Boot, E. ...	... ...	0	5 0
Flanagan, Mrs., Sen.	...	0	5 0
Coman, J....	... ...	0	5 0
Walter, E....	... ...	0	5 0
Harkas, W.	... ...	0	5 0
Tier, B. ...	... ...	0	5 0
Sums under 5s....	... ...	0	15 0

MUDGEE.

Bayly, N. P., J.P., "Havi- lah"	... ...	5	0 0
Cox, Hon. G. H., M.L.C. "Burrandulla"	... ...	2	2 0
Watt, D., Pine Ridge, Dennison Town	... ...	2	0 0
Cox, Alex. H., J.P....	...	2	0 0
Rowling, Dr.	... ...	1	1 0
Gellatley, J. C....	... ...	1	1 0
Lowe, W. H., "Eurun- derce"	... ...	1	1 0
Lawson, C. W., J.P., "Putta Bucca"	... ...	1	0 0

	£	s	d
Gunther, Rev. Archdeacon	1	0	0
Schlachter, F.	1	0	0
Crossing, G.	1	0	0
Lester, W. R.	1	0	0
Lowe, C. B., J.P., "Goorce"	1	0	0
Lowe, R., J.P., "Wilbetree"	1	0	0
Cadell, Mrs., "Mullamuddy"	1	0	0
Atkinson, James	1	0	0
Blackman, W. R., J.P. ...	1	0	0
Dowling, Vincent,"Lowcu" Rylston...	1	0	0
Hellmann, J.	1	0	0
Stacy, B.	0	10	6
McEwan, Rev. A.	0	10	6
Bourne, J. C.	0	10	6
Moses, S. S.	0	10	6
Clarke, E....	0	10	6
Greenwood, E. J.	0	10	6
Meares, C. D.	0	10	6
White, R. H. D., J.P. ...	0	10	0
Hinton, J....	0	10	0
Crossing, Mrs., "Enfield"	0	10	0
Victoria Brewery	0	10	0
Newton, Dr. J. L.	0	10	0
Davidson, G.	0	10	0
Browne, DeCourcy	0	10	0
Western Post	0	6	0
Meares, W. D., P.M. ...	0	5	0
Daly, E.	0	5	0
Millett, W. W...	0	5	0
Beattie, A.	0	5	0
Hazlestine, G.	0	5	0
Branscombe, W.	0	5	0
Caldwell, Rev. R.	0	5	0
Wood, W. F.	0	5	0
Bishop, W.	0	5	0
Sheppard, M. J.	0	5	0
Nichilson, W. L.	0	5	0
Mudgee Independent ...	0	4	0
Sums under 5s....	0	11	0
Western Post, Advertisements half price			

MURRUMBURRAH.

	£	s	d
Macansh, J., J.P., "Garangula"	2	0	0
Harris, W. M....	1	1	0
Barnes, T. and G.	1	1	0
A Friend	0	10	0
Davies, Captain T. A., J.P. "Naut Gwylan"... ...	0	10	0
Donkin, J. B., J.P., "Nimbey"	0	10	0

	£	s	d
Dillon, Mrs.	0	10	0
A Friend...	0	5	0
Murphy, M.	0	5	0
Cutcliffe, C., B.A., C.P.S.	0	5	0
Reid, D.	0	5	0
Passmore, J.	0	5	0
McGee, Sen. Ser	0	5	0
Graham, W.	0	5	0
A Friend...	0	5	0
Aikin, A....	0	5	0
Bourne, J...	0	5	0
Sums under 5s...	0	5	0

NIMITYBELL.

	£	s	d
Driscoll, John, "Summer Hill"	0	10	6
McKeaohie, Capt. "Mount Cooper"	0	10	0
Johuson, T.	0	5	0
Selk, O. E.	0	5	0
Graham, W.	0	5	0
Sums under 5s...	0	2	0
Ditto per favor of J. Mc Kee, Royal Hotel, Collected by	1	10	0

ORANGE.

	£	s	d
Moulder, W. N.	1	1	0
Whitney, W. F.	1	1	0
Codrington, J. F.	1	1	0
Nesson Brothers	1	1	0
Bowen, M. B.	1	1	0
Smith, J. W.	1	1	0
Rotton, Mrs., "Kangaroobie"	1	1	0
Fisher, E....	1	0	0
Gain, J. H.	1	0	0
Kerr, A. T., J.P.	1	0	0
Frost, R.	1	0	0
Evans, W. T., C.P.S. ...	0	10	6
Nathan, E.	0	10	6
Clayton, R.	0	10	0
Scarr, Percy	0	10	0
Dale, W., J.P....	0	10	0
Davies, E. C. and Co. ...	0	10	0
Boyce, Rev. F. B.	0	10	0
Poultou, J. B.	0	10	0
Waddell, G. M.	0	10	0
Warren, W.	0	10	0
Brooke, J....	0	10	0
Dwyer, J....	0	10	0
McLachlan, J. C.	0	10	0
Grassick, J.	0	10	0
Kiuna, P., Mayor	0	10	0

	£	s	d
McClymont, J.	0	10	0
Towson, G.	0	10	0
Torpy, J.	0	10	0
Keegan, M.	0	5	0
Eccles, A.	0	5	0
Adams, J. H.	0	5	0
Nolan, Rev. J. A.	0	5	0
Strachan Brothers	0	5	0
Parker, J.	0	5	0
Withers, J.	0	5	0
" Verox "	0	5	0
Laughton, Rev. J. B.	0	5	0
Giugni, M.	0	5	0
Goddard, F.	0	5	0
Windred, J.	0	5	0
Stynes, R.	0	5	0
Stockwell, C.	0	5	0
Dale, James, J.P.	0	5	0
Jackson, A.	0	5	0
Larance, H. W.	0	5	0
Whiteford, R. J.	0	5	0
Morrison, G. W.	0	5	0
Paul, J. M.	0	5	0
Higmann, J.	0	5	0
Sums under 5s	0	10	0

PAMBULA.

	£	s	d
Cameron, Mrs.	0	10	0
McKee, D.	0	10	0
Baddeley, C. H., J.P.	0	10	0
Wellings, T. H.	0	5	0
Doherty, P.	0	5	0
Behl, J.	0	5	0
Pryke, J.	0	5	0
Haywood, J.	0	5	0
Chapel, Mrs.	0	5	0
Bray, T.	0	5	0
Davis, G. F.	0	5	0
Sums under 5s	0	3	6

QUEANBEYAN.

	£	s	d
Russell, Colonel, P.M.	1	1	0
Wright, J. J., J.P.	1	1	0
Ware, Rev. J., Maitland	1	1	0
Nugent, J. W.	1	0	0
Cunningham, A. and J., "Laynon"	1	0	0
O'Neill, W. G.	0	10	6
McKellar, R. W.	0	10	6
Willans, O., C.P.S.	0	10	6
Mehogan, Mrs. R.	0	10	6
Bull, J.	0	10	0
Gale, J., *Queanbeyan Age*	0	10	0
Byrne, M., J.P.	0	5	0

	£	s	d
Parr, T.	0	5	0
Walker, J. H. W.	0	5	0
Scott, C.	0	5	0
Hunt, W.	0	5	0
Lough, E. P.	0	5	0
Brennan, Sen. Sergeant	0	5	0
Kealman, J.	0	5	0
Laing, T. H.	0	5	0
Hollitt, W.	0	5	0
Pooley, Mrs. M.	0	5	0
Van Heythaysen, R.	0	5	0
Myers, A.	0	5	0
Sums under 5s	1	2	6

SEYMOUR.

	£	s	d
Harnett, Mrs. Mary, "Eucumbene"	1	0	0
Barrett, A., J.P.	0	10	0
Delaney, J., "Buckenday"	0	10	0
Melville, G. F.	0	10	0
McKay, S.	0	10	0
Hoskins, W.	0	10	0
Barrett, H.	0	5	0
Oulds, Thomas	0	5	0
Gaulway, E.	0	5	0
Berigan, J. W.	0	5	0
Conolly, T.	0	5	0
Conuolly, Thomas	0	5	0
Sums under 5s	0	4	6

SHELLHARBOUR.

	£	s	d
Wilson, Captain	0	10	0
Redhall, T. A., J.P.	0	10	0
Dunster, W. and H.	0	10	0
Dunster, Mrs. J.	0	10	0
Wilson, R.	0	8	0
Coughran, Mrs.	0	5	0
Allen, Mrs.	0	5	0
Barrs, Miss	0	5	0
Condon, D.	0	5	0
Hall, R.	0	5	0
Lindsley, Mrs. D.	0	5	0
Sums under 5s	0	8	0

SHOALHAVEN.

	£	s	d
Berry, D., "Coolangatta"	1	1	0
Morton, H. G., J.P.	1	1	0
McArthur and Co.	0	10	6
Weller, J.	0	5	0
Morrow, J. R.	0	5	0
Bennie, J.	0	5	0
Pooley, E.	0	5	0
Marrack, M.	0	5	0
Tory, G.	0	5	0

Morison, Mrs.	£0	5	0
Green, J., Mayor	0	5	0
Graham, C.	0	5	0
Sums under 5s...	0	5	6
Shoalhaven News, Advertisements free			

TUMUT.

McKay, R.	3	12	0
Brown, E. G., J.P.	1	1	0
Tingcombe, H. C.	1	1	0
Forsyth, G., J.P., " Yarrongobilly "	1	1	0
Vyner, F. W., P.M... ...	1	0	0
Marks, W. B., J.P.... ...	1	0	0
Marks, M....	1	0	0
Millar, D., " The Elms "...	1	0	0
Spencer, Rev. G.	1	0	0
Newman and Co.	1	0	0
Swift, S. M.	1	0	0
Robertson, J.	0	10	6
Wilson, T.	0	10	6
Donnelly, M.	0	10	6
Quilty, M....	0	10	6
Lynch, Dr...	0	10	0
Caspersonn, Mrs. L.... ...	0	10	0
Bridle, W. H.	0	10	0
Robinson, Mrs., Sen. ...	0	10	0
Cooke, Mrs.	0	10	0
Simmons, J.	0	10	0
Shelley, R. M.	0	5	0
Bridle, Mrs.	0	5	0
Bridle, Miss M.	0	5	0
A Friend	0	5	0
Bax, W.	0	5	0
Bridle, W. H.	0	5	0
Piper, A., Sen....	0	5	0
Rankin, Mrs. N.	0	5	0
Alexander, J.	0	5	0
McKenzie, K. C.	0	5	0
Howard, G.	0	5	0
Tuohy, M.	0	5	0
McNamara, N....	0	5	0
Emery, D. J.	0	5	0
Weeden, J.	0	5	0
Sums under 5s...	0	3	6
Tumut and Adelong Times Advertisements free ...			

ULLADULLA.

Sturrock, W.	1	0	0
Wheatley, Mrs...	0	10	0
Cashman, W.	0	10	0
Millard, W. and G.... ...	0	10	0
Mackenzie, K.	0	5	0

Seccombe, E.	£0	5	0
Fitch, C.	0	5	0
Taylor, P....	0	5	0
Gambell, Mrs.	0	5	0
Sums under 5s...	0	2	0

WAGGA WAGGA.

Smith, Alex., " Kyambia "	5	0	0
Tompson, E. H., C.P.S. 1877-8	2	2	0
Tompson, Mr. & Mrs. F. A.	2	2	0
Garland, J. R., 1877-8 ...	2	2	0
Bolton, A. T., 1877-8 ...	2	2	0
Croker, C. H.	1	1	0
Bolton, C. F.	1	1	0
Wren, Dr.	1	1	0
Fitzhardinge, H. B... ...	1	1	0
Campbell and Campbell...	1	1	0
Roberts, Copeland & Co...	1	1	0
Leitch, J., J.P., " Berry Jerry "	1	1	0
Wollman, Mrs....	1	1	0
Monks, A. J.	1	1	0
Jones, A. G., J.P.	1	1	0
Bonynge, T.	1	1	0
Donnelly, E. W., " Berambule "	1	0	0
Pownall, Rev. Archdeacon	1	0	0
Roper, F.	1	0	0
Edmondson, J. S.	1	0	0
Gibbs, W. B., "Carrabosh"	1	0	0
Donnelly, J.	1	0	0
Commins, G. W.	1	0	0
Gordon, J.	1	0	0
Mackay, A.	1	0	0
Mair, G., J.P., Mayor ...	0	10	6
Nixon, R.	0	10	6
Tompson, C. J...	0	10	6
Korff, F.	0	10	0
Gowland, F. W.	0	10	0
Scott, W.	0	10	0
Faulkner, Mrs...	0	10	0
Goodisson, R. G.	0	10	0
Shaw, E.	0	10	0
Moran, P....	0	10	0
Macarthur, W...	0	10	0
Chapman, J. W.	0	10	0
Rand, E.	0	10	0
Rand, W., J.P...	0	10	0
L. A. F.	0	10	0
Minnett, E.	0	5	0
J. F.	0	5	0
Schmidt, W.	0	5	0
Howard, R.	0	5	0

		£ s. d.
J. E. C.	...	£0 5 0
Sums under 5s... ...	...	0 5 0
Wagga Express Advertisements free		

WELLINGTON.

		£ s. d.
Gardiner, J. A., "Gobolion"		1 1 0
Bravey, Rev. J. C.		1 0 0
Smith, E. A.,"Narroogal"		1 0 0
Marsh, F., J.P.		0 10 0
Pantlin, G. H....		0 10 0
Bayly, J.		0 10 0
Way, W. G.		0 10 0
Matthews, E. J.		0 10 0
Woodly, F. W.		0 10 0
Rygate, Dr., J.P.		0 9 0
O'Connell, D.		0 6 0
Daniel, Mrs.		0 5 0
Forwood, W. H.		0 5 0
Barton, C. H.		0 5 0
Shewen, Dr.		0 5 0
Turner, A. W....		0 5 0
Chauncy, W. S.		0 5 0
Sums under 5s...		0 4 6
Wellington Gazette Advertisements free		

WOLLONGONG.

		£ s. d.
Osborne, Miss, per F. P. McCabe...		5 0 0
Osborne, G., J.P., "Foxlow" Bungendore ...		1 1 0
Bright, J.		1 1 0
Woodward, F....		1 1 0
Robertson, W. G.		0 10 0
Wilson, W.		0 10 0
Brown, Rev. J., Walkden		0 10 0
Osborne, W.		0 10 0
Cole, F. K.		0 10 0
Turner, A. A., P.M... ...		0 10 0
Campbell and Hart... ...		0 10 0
Ewing, Rev. T. C.		0 10 0
Davis, Mrs.		0 10 0
Hosking, J. W...		0 5 0
Griffin, Mrs., Sen.		0 5 0
Marr, H.		0 5 0
Parsons, R.		0 5 0
Beatson, A.		0 5 0
Young, J....		0 5 0
Parsons, A.		0 5 0
Pike, Mrs....		0 5 0
Brown, C....		0 5 0
Armstrong, A., Mayor ...		0 5 0

		£ s. d.
Wiseman, W. J.		£0 5 0
Griffin, D., Jun.		0 5 0
Jones, E. A.		0 5 0
McDonald, D.		0 5 0
Jones, Tom		0 5 0
Wilmot, J.		0 5 0
Spence, W. M....		0 5 0
Sums under 5s...		1 2 6

WOMBAT.

		£ s. d.
Ekins, C. H.		0 5 0
Lewington, C. P.		0 5 0
Yerbury, Mrs.		0 5 0
Sums under 5s...		0 7 6

YASS.

		£ s. d.
Barber, T., J.P., 1877-78		2 2 0
Yates, L., P.M.		1 1 0
Iceton, E. A.		1 1 0
Wilkinson, W. F.		1 1 0
Pearson, R. W.		1 1 0
Johnson, R. P., "Jeir" ...		1 1 0
Ritchie, J. P.		1 1 0
Sharp, J. B., J.P.		1 1 0
Lawson, G.		1 0 0
Mallyon, J. H. P.		1 0 0
Hume, Mrs. Hamilton ...		1 0 0
O'Brien, Mrs. H.		1 0 0
Yarrington, Rev. W. H....		0 10 6
Macintosh, R. C.		0 10 6
Morris, Rev. R. Newton...		0 10 6
Morris, Alfred A.		0 10 6
Yeo, J. C....		0 10 6
McBean, Springmount ...		0 10 6
Clayton, Mrs.		0 10 6
Dodds, H....		0 10 6
Leathart, F.		0 10 0
Perry, M., J.P., Mayor ...		0 10 0
Glasson, Rev. G. R. ...		0 10 0
Mote, T.		0 10 0
Walton, L.		0 10 0
Jones, Rees		0 10 0
Williams, J. G. L., J.P....		0 10 0
Bernston, D.		0 5 0
Colls, J. R.		0 5 0
Gardiner, J.		0 5 0
Maltby, Mrs.		0 5 0
Barry, J.		0 5 0
Howard, F.		0 5 0
Comins, W.		0 5 0
Ayling, T....		0 5 0
Allman, Mrs.		0 5 0
Crago, P. T.		0 5 0
Pearse, E. E.		0 5 0

McDonogh, J.	£0	5	0	Robison, Hugh...	£1	0	0
Buckland, J.	0	5	0	Marina, Carlo, "Moppity"	1	0	0
Sums under 5s...	0	10	0	Robinson, S., P.M.	1	0	0
Yass Courier Advertise-				*Burrangong Argus*	0	10	6
ments free				*Ditto Chronicle*	0	10	6
Hannam, J., "Cooradig-				Caldwell, S., Jun., "Eu-			
bee," Bookham	1	1	0	rabba"	0	10	6
Drummond, Alex., ditto...	0	10	0	Seaborn, Rev. R.	0	10	0
Sheahan, Mrs., Jugiong ...	0	13	0	Salmon, J. B.	0	10	0
				Freestone, A. S.	0	10	0
YOUNG.				Heeley, Dr.	0	10	0
				Sharp, W....	0	10	0
Foster, Teather T. B. ...	2	2	0	Mackenzie Brothers ...	0	10	0
Scarvell, E. A....	1	1	0	Meares, J. D.	0	10	0
Bell, Sydney	1	1	0	A Friend	0	5	0
Watson Brothers	1	1	0	Fuller, F.	0	5	0
Honour, A. W.	1	1	0	A Friend	0	5	0
Tucker, C. T.	1	1	0	A Friend	0	5	0
Russell, J....	1	1	0	A Friend	0	5	0
Clarke, G. O. M., J.P. ...	1	0	0	Minter, H.	0	5	0
Cram, P.	1	0	0	Sums under 5s...	0	5	6

NOTE.—Any subscription not appearing in this list will be found in the GENERAL LIST, page 22.

QUEENSLAND,

Per Mr. W. B. STEVENS.

——+—⟨∞⟩—+——

ALLORA.

Clark, C., East Talgi	.. £1	0	0
Campbell, Rev. H. J.	... 0	10	0
Gordon, S.	0	5	0
Cranitch, P.	0	5	0
Burge, W.	0	5	0
Kennedy, T.	0	5	0
Deacon, W., Mayor ...	0	5	0
Cook, R.	0	5	0
Hendon, Station Master...	0	5	0
Myers, J. H. C.	0	2	6

BRISBANE.

Kennedy, His Excellency Sir A. E., K.C.M.G., C.B.	5	0	0
Palmer, Hon. A.H., M.L.A.	3	3	0
Griffith, Hon. S. W., M.L.A.	2	2	0
Morehead, Hon. D. B., M.L.A.	2	2	0
Brown, D. L. and Co. ...	2	2	0
Raff and Co., G.	2	2	0
Stewart and Hemmant ...	2	2	0
Brown, Hon. A. H., M.L.C.	2	0	0
Bishop of Brisbane, Right Rev. Lord	2	2	0
Lilley, Mr. Justice	2	2	0
Walsh, W. H., M.L.A. ...	2	2	0
Raff, A., J.P.	2	2	0
Chapman, E., (1877-78.)...	3	0	0
Dickson, Hon. J. R., M.L.A.	2	2	0
Edmondstom, Hon. G., M.L.C.	2	0	0
Mein, Hon. C. S.	1	1	0
Martin, A., J.P.	1	1	0
Butler Bros.	1	1	0
Murphy, W. E.	1	1	0
Bramston, H., J.P.	1	1	0

Fraser, S., M.L.A. £1	1	0
Shaw, A. and Co.	1	1	0
McPherson, P....	1	10	0
Brabant and Co.	1	1	0
Barnett, E. and Co.... ...	1	1	0
Carmichael, L.	1	1	0
Scott, Dawson and Stewart	1	1	0
Armour, R. L.	1	1	0
Watson and Ferguson ...	1	1	0
Miles, Hon. W., M.L.A....	1	1	0
Williams, W.	1	1	0
Manwairn, J. S., and employees	1	10	0
Quinlan Gray and Co. ...	1	1	0
Chambers, A. W.	1	1	0
Beattie, F., M.L.A.... ...	1	1	0
Lukin, G. L., J.P.	1	1	0
Pettigrew, W., M.L.C. ...	1	1	0
Little and Brown	1	1	0
Bale, J. L.	1	1	0
Flavelle Bros. & Roberts...	1	1	0
Sinclair, D., S. Brisbane...	1	1	0
McGhee, Luya and Co. ...	1	1	0
Wyborn, Captain	1	1	0
Wilson, F. W. and Co. ...	1	1	0
Heath, Captain, R. N. ...	1	1	0
Stanley, H. C.	1	1	0
Potts, Paul and Sargent ...	1	1	0
Brown, W. J.	1	1	0
Thorn, W.	1	1	0
Wakefield, H.	1	1	0
Myers, G. and Company...	1	1	0
Mort, Holland and Co. ...	1	1	0
Smellie, R. R.	1	1	0
Butler, W., Kilcoy	1	1	0
Hubbard, A., Mayor ...	1	0	0
Phillips, P.	1	0	0
Oxley, H. J.	1	0	0
Fletcher, C.	1	0	0
Swan, James, M.L.C. ...	1	0	0

Quinn, Bishop	...	...	£1	0	0	Jordan, M.	£0 10	0
Burns, John	...	...	1	0	0	Castsons, F. W. A.	0 10	0
Row, R. H., M.A.	...	...	1	0	0	Gibson, Mrs. A.	0 10	0
Drury, E. R., J.P.	...	...	1	0	0	Wark, S.	0 5	0
Petrie, J., J.P.	...	...	1	0	0	Harris, M...	0 5	0
Tully, W. A., J.P.	...	...	1	0	0	Castsons, G.	0 5	0
Whish, Capt. C. B.	...	...	1	0	0	Hall, W.	0 5	0
Goggs, M., Goodna	...	...	1	0	0	McGoldrick, A...	0 5	0
Perry, W....	...	...	1	0	0	Sums under 5s...	0 3	0
Honeyman, J.	...	...	1	0	0			
Molle, G. B. and Co.	...	...	1	0	0	FELTON STATION,		
Telegraph office	...	...	0	16	0	Tyson, J., J.P....	5 0	0
Patriot office ...	...	...	0	12	0	Donely and Hewitt	2 0	0
Berkley and Taylor...	...	...	0	10	6	Whitchurch, F.	0 5	0
Ward, M., J.P.... ...	...	...	0	10	6	Station Master, Cambooya	0 5	0
Finney and Isles	...	...	0	10	6			
Harrison, G. D.	...	...	0	10	6	GOWRIE STATION.		
Ellis, J. B.	...	...	0	10	6	King, G., J.P.	2 2	0
Woodcock, F. ...	...	...	0	10	0	King, G. B.	1 1	0
Boyde, A., Mitton	...	...	0	10	0	King, H. V.	1 1	0
Griffith, Rev. E.	...	...	0	10	0			
McNaught, J. W.	...	...	0	10	0	GYMPIE.		
Aitchison, W.	...	...	0	10	0			
Cameron, John...	...	...	0	10	0	Couldery, W. F.	1 1	0
Hill, Walter	...	...	0	10	0	Elworthy, John	1 1	0
Keith, W... ...	...	...	0	5	0	Humphreys, Rev. S. ...	1 0	0
McNab, D.	...	...	0	5	0	McDonald, A.	0 10	6
Snow, Brothers...	...	...	0	5	0	Ferguson, W.	0 10	0
Moxley, T. C. ...	...	...	0	5	0	Black, A.	0 10	0
Longlands, D. F.	...	...	0	5	0	Mure, G. G.	0 10	0
						Telfor, F.	0 10	0
DALBY.						Kennedy, R.	0 10	0
Landy Brothers	...	...	1	1	0·	Cox and Roberts	0 10	0
Simpson, G. M., Bon						Sums under 5s.	0 2	6
Accord Station	...	...	1	1	0			
O'Brien, D.	...	...	1	0	0	IPSWICH.		
Mohoupt, H.	...	...	1	0	0	Cribb and Foote	5 5	0
Evans, A. H., St. Ruth	...		1	0	0	Proprietor of the Ipswich		
Cory, Mrs. G. G., Cecil						Observer	1 8	0
Plains	...	...	1	0	0	Cameron, D.	1 1	0
Brodribb, and Co., Kurro-						Cannan, J. K.	1 1	0
wah	...	...	1	0	0	Wilson, G. H. and Co. ...	1 1	0
Wilkie, G., St. Ruth	...		0	10	0	Hughes and Cameron ..	1 1	0
Lowrie, Rev. J.	...	...	0	10	0	Tallon, R., J.P....	1 1	0
Malaham, Rev. R. ...	...	...	0	10	0	Myers and Isambert ...	1 1	0
Callaghan, J. ...	...	...	0	10	0	Wilson, Mrs. G. H.... ...	1 1	0
Oswald, J. D. ...	...	...	0	10	0	Von Lossberg, Dr., J.P. ...	1 1	0
Merreth, F.	...	...	0	10	0	Proprietors of the Queens-		
Jessop, J. S.	...	...	0	10	0	land Times	1 1	0
Good, T. C.	...	...	0	10	0	Daisey, M.	1 0	0
Conroy, J... ...	...	...	0	10	0	Foote, J., M.L.A.	1 0	0
Donald, R... ...	...	...	0	10	0	Thorn, Mrs.	1 0	0
McIntosh, A. ...	...	...	0	10	0	Ivory, J., M.L.A.	1 0	0
Benjamin, S., and Co.	...		0	10	0	Whitehouse, F.	0 10	6

Francis, J., Mayor	£0 10	6
Gibson, J.	0 10	6
Cameron, Gorden	0 10	6
Vowles, W.	0 10	6
Hoey, T. W.	0 10	0
Brady, T. W.	0 10	0
Lyons, T. B.	0 10	0
Shenton, S., J.P.	0 10	0
Greenham and Co.	0 10	0
Henderson, Mrs. J.	0 10	0
Sweeny, P.	0 10	0
Gill, R.	0 10	0
McFarland and Son ...	0 10	0
Darvall, A.	0 10	0
Kennedy, Dr. N. J.	0 10	0
North, Rev. Roger	0 10	0
Powell, B.	0 10	0
McGarth, J.	0 7	6
Tatham, W.	0 5	0
Kendall, R. J.	0 5	0
Heeney, J.	0 5	0
Hockley, J. and Co. ...	0 5	0
Bowers, M.	0 5	0
Fleischman, J. F.	0 5	0
Real, M.	0 5	0
O'Malley, M., C.P.S. ...	0 5	0
McGill, J.	0 5	0
Halley, J.	0 5	0
Towell, T.	0 5	0
Zillman, Rev. M.	0 5	0
Ware, G.	0 5	0
Brown, W.	0 5	0
Goff, Z.	0 5	0
Gorry, C., J.P	0 5	0

Employees of Cribb and Foote—

Young, H. A.	0 10	0
North, J.	0 10	0
Cribb, T. B.	0 10	6
Cribb, Joseph and James	0 10	0
McGill, James	0 5	0
Phair, E.	0 2	6
Grigg, G. F.	0 2	6
Rose, J.	0 2	6
Grigson, W.	0 5	0
Barrymore, F. W.	0 2	6
Hutchinson, James	0 2	6
Foote, A. M.	0 5	0
Comport, Charles	0 2	6
Tacry, W. T.	0 2	0
Ivett, J.	0 5	0
Payne, E.	0 2	6
McGill, J. W.	0 2	6
Tomes, H.	0 2	6
Ross, Thomas	0 2	6

Boyle, T.	£0 5	0
Birglar, F.	0 2	6
Greene, S.	0 2	6
Danley, H.	0 2	6
Bourke, J. G.	0 2	6
A Friend	0 2	6
T. W. B.	0 2	0

Employees on Ipswich Railway
works—

Horinblow, H.	0 10	0
Ainscon, J.	0 5	0
Evans, H.	0 2	6
Foreman, Thomas	0 2	6
Johnson, W.	0 2	0
Beard, Edward	0 5	0
Blyth, A.	0 2	6
McCarroll, S.	0 2	6
Webb, James	0 5	0
Meldrum, W.	0 5	0
Suett, J.	0 5	0
Bailey, A.	0 2	6
Elliott, John	0 2	0
Harris, W.	0 2	6
Scriven, W.	0 2	6
Holt, John	0 2	6
May, A.	0 2	6
McGill, W.	0 2	6
Young, John	0 2	0
Hill, J. W.	0 2	0
King, Thomas	0 2	6
Marshall, E.	0 2	0
Mensforth, J.	0 2	0
De Calmer, J.	0 2	6
Phillips, S.	0 2	6
Bowling, J.	0 2	6
Pettigrew, J.	0 5	0
Pearse, J.	0 5	0
Owen, J.	0 2	6
Bruckner, H.	0 2	6
Hellawell, J. B.	0 2	6
Brassey, E.	0 2	6
Ruddle, J.	0 2	6
Waters, G.	0 2	6
Coey, O.	0 2	6
Springall, F. G.	0 2	6
Robinson, J.	0 2	6
McCrae, J.	0 5	0
Bassey, F.	0 2	0
Ogier, W.	0 2	0
Ogden, W.	0 2	0
Fries, W.	0 2	0
Rose, J.	0 5	0
Barber, W. E.	0 2	6
Eagle, W. H.	0 2	6

	£	s	d
Geller, G.	£0	2	6
Hadley, H.	0	2	6
Cramer, F.	0	2	6
Both, J.	0	2	6
Fischer, R.	0	2	6
Larter, F.	0	2	6
Lovell, W.	0	2	6
Swan, J.	0	2	6
Gall, W.	0	2	6
Saulsbury, J.	0	2	6
Foote, A.	0	2	6
Cook, W.	0	2	6
Morrow, J.	0	2	6
Thomas, W.	0	2	6
Thomas, P.	0	2	6
Findley, R.	0	2	6
Martin, J.	0	1	0
Flinn, Thomas	0	2	6
Mills, W. H.	0	2	6
Riddel, Thomas	0	2	0
McCaskie, E.	0	2	6
Freeman, Thomas	0	2	0
Wynne, A.	0	2	6
Turner, E.	0	2	6
Williams, D.	0	2	6
Drew, A.	0	2	6
Davis, W.	0	2	0
Popham, Charles	0	2	6
Stephenson, S.	0	5	0
McDonald, W.	0	2	0
Hegarty, C.	0	2	0
Johns, H.	0	1	0
Sagar, A.	0	5	0
Bagried, W.	0	2	6

JONDARYAN STATION.

	£	s	d
Williams, Charles, J.P. ...	2	2	0
Beardmore, G. O., Oakey Creek	1	0	0
Tully, Margaret	0	10	0
Mirchinn, F.	0	10	0
Hodgson, W.	0	5	0
Beauclerc, F. C.	0	10	0
Schell, J.	0	10	0
Flannagan, D).	0	5	0
Wyatt, H.	0	5	0
Arnold, F.	0	5	0
McGoverin, B.	0	5	0
Hodgson, G.	0	5	0
Wharf, A. M.	0	4	0
Fillsley, R.	0	2	6
Schutle, F.	0	2	6
Evans, Mrs.	0	2	6
Walker, A.	0	2	0

	£	s	d
Miers, J.	£0	5	0
Friends	2	18	6

MARYBOROUGH.

	£	s	d
Hyne, R. M., Mayor ...	2	2	0
Noaks, J. E., J.P.	2	2	0
Walker, John, and Co. ...	2	2	0
Wilson, Hart and Co. ...	2	2	0
Graham, John	1	1	0
Woodrow and Co.	1	1	0
Williams, W.	1	1	0
Miller, Menzie...	1	1	0
Falkner, J.	1	1	0
Powell, C.	1	1	0
Boge, M.	1	1	0
Gray, H. S.	1	1	0
Baker, T.	1	1	0
Pettigrew, W., and Co. ...	1	1	0
Gataker, C. F.	1	1	0
Gilbert and Co.	1	1	0
Graham and Co.	1	1	0
Annear and Co...	1	1	0
Roberts, W. S.	1	1	0
Cadell, J. J.	1	0	0
Palmer, H.	1	0	0
Tooth and Cran, Yangarie	1	0	0
Mirls, T.	0	10	6
Walker, W.	0	10	6
Hughes, C.	0	10	6
Hornsburgh, J...	0	10	6
Lyons and Powell	0	10	6
Corset and Morton	0	10	6
Hornsburgh G., and Co...	0	10	6
Williams, W. H.	0	10	6
Jones, R.	0	10	0
Cane Brothers	0	10	0
Tooth, N.	0	10	0
Blanchard, J.	0	10	0
Finch, E. J.	0	10	0
Blue, N.	0	10	0
Fairlie and Son	0	10	0
Brennen and Geraghty ...	0	10	0
Fulton, J.	0	10	0
Bliss, J. H.	0	10	0
Irving, W. H.	0	10	0
Appin, John	0	10	0
A Friend	0	5	0
Stupart, G.	0	5	0
Wearin, J.	0	5	0
Young, John	0	5	0
Hobson, E. J.	0	5	0
Royle and Son	0	5	0
Baynbam, W.	0	5	0
A Friend	0	5	0

	£	s	d
Brott, J.	£0	5	0
Gibson, J.	0	5	0
Barbeler, V.	0	5	0
Vogel, X.	0	5	0
O'Brien, J.	0	5	0
Mannix, M. H....	0	5	0
McMah, R.	0	5	0
Graham, James	0	5	0
Sums under 5s....	0	5	0

Collected by E. Armitage, Mungar
Saw Mills.—

	£	s	d
E. A. 10s., M. Nugent 5s.	0	15	0
J. H. 5s., Malbra, G. 5s.	0	10	0
Peat, Y. P.	0	5	0
Atkinson, George	0	5	0
Allen, T.	0	5	0
Martin, John	0	5	0
McCoy, Charles	0	5	0
Fentimae, S.	0	5	0
Srendsen, J.	0	5	0
Hasdy, N....	0	5	0
Higgins, J.	0	5	0
Christison, J.	0	5	0
Crawford, Thomas G. ...	0	5	0
Edge, J. G.	0	5	0
Sums under 5s....	1	7	6

ROCKHAMPTON.

	£	s	d
Jackson, W. G., Mayor ...	2	2	0
Reid, Walter	2	2	0
Headrick and Co.	2	2	0
Stewart and Lucas	2	2	0
McFarland, John, M.L.A.	2	2	0
Saber Brothers	1	1	0
Hopkins, William	1	1	0
Pattison, W.	1	1	0
Tuson, G....	1	1	0
Achieson and Allen... ...	1	1	0
Walton, W. F....	1	1	0
Willson, Hart and Co. ...	1	1	0
Jones, Rees R....	1	1	0
Feez, A.	1	1	0
Rhodes, J.	1	1	0
Budden, T. F....	1	1	0
Harden, C.	1	1	0
Martin, A.	1	1	0
Nemo	1	1	0
Woods and Woods	1	1	0
Higson, W.	1	1	0
Face, J. W.	1	1	0
Jones, Thomas and Co. ...	1	1	0
Curtis, G. S.	1	1	0
Callaghan, W....	1	1	0
Shaw, G. B.	1	1	0

	£	s	d
Isles, Finney and Co. ...	£1	0	0
Hall, T. S...	1	0	0
Sandel, L....	1	0	0
Ferguson, John	1	0	0
Downer, P.	0	10	6
Orr, J. F.	0	10	6
Faunce, T. F.	0	10	6
Hill, S. G., C.P.S.	0	10	6
Forrest, J.	0	10	0
Thozet, A.	0	10	0
Roberts, T. P.	0	10	0
Kingel, Mrs.	0	10	0
Jones, G. H.	0	10	0
Peterson, D.	0	10	0
Bredfeldt, E.	0	10	0
Caporn, W. G...	0	10	0
Kasch and Jargin	0	10	0
Cruickshank, R. D.	0	10	0
Daglish, J. and D.	0	8	0
Scanlan, J...	0	5	0
Cahill, J.	0	5	0
Irwin, T.	0	5	0
Bones Brothers...	0	5	0
Merson, J...	0	5	0
O'Rouke, J., Comit	1	0	0
McLaughlin, T.	1	1	0
MeSherry, J.	1	0	0
Leivsley, W.	0	10	0
Pavis, J.	0	5	0
Sheeley, W., Blackwater	0	10	0
Cherry and Gibson	0	5	0
Sums under 5s...	0	2	6

Advertisements free in the
Morning Bulletin... ...

STANTHORPE.

	£	s	d
Dennis, J....	1	10	0
Tyrel, JohnDePoix,M.L.A.	1	1	0
Westhoven, C. G.	1	1	0
Greenup, A.	1	0	0
Barton, A....	0	10	0
Gilham, W. G....	0	5	0
Howell, W.	0	5	0

YANDILLA STATION.

	£	s	d
Gore and Co.	2	2	0
Gore, F. R.	1	1	0
Gore, G. R.	1	1	0
Gore, R. W.	1	1	0
Hopkins, E. B....	1	1	0
Caroll, J.	1	0	0
Ballie, Mrs. John	1	0	0
Fitzmaurice, George R. ...	0	10	6
Hodgkinson, Dr. E.... ...	0	10	6

	£	s	d
Purcell, J. P.	0	10	6
Brown, Mrs. John	0	10	0
McGowan, Nicholas ...	0	10	0
Robertson, Mrs.	0	10	0
Law, Professor H.	0	5	0
Dowling, Patrick	0	5	0
Brown, Sarah	0	5	0
Bleakley, Ellen...	0	5	0
Ah Ken	0	5	0
Ah Chow	0	5	0
Duffus, Robert	0	5	0
Dayer, James	0	5	0
Lee, James	0	5	0
Williams, Edward, J.P. ...	0	5	0
Quack, Peter	0	5	0
Donald, S. B.	0	2	6
Bougard, Eliza...	0	2	6

TOOWOOMBA.

	£	s	d
Taylor, Hon. James ...	2	2	0
Beer, J. and W.	1	1	0
Aland, R.	1	1	0
Campbell, J. C. and W. ...	1	1	0
Robinson, E. W., J.P. ...	1	1	0
Cribb, B., P.M	1	1	0
Roberts, Dr. E.	1	1	0
Caswell, H. D....	1	0	0
Holberton, F. H., J.P ...	1	0	0
Blackburn, J.	0	7	6
Benjamin, D. and J. ...	0	10	6
Filsher, R.	0	10	0
Pechey, E. W...	0	10	6
McKenzie, J. P.	0	10	6
Glanvelle, G. W.	0	10	0
Walker, C. E.	0	10	0
Boyce, J. A., C.P.S. ...	0	10	0
Cobb, J. Ashgrove	0	10	0
McIntrye, J. S.	0	10	0
Stevens, H. and Co. ...	0	10	0
Garget, J., Mayor	0	10	0
Abraham, Rev. T.	0	10	0
McLeish, Booth and Co...	0	10	0
Wooldridge, A.	0	10	0
Meagher, Miss...	0	10	0
Ruthning, H. L. E.... ...	0	10	0
Stevens, S. G.	0	10	0
Ross and Taylor	0	10	0
Wilcox, E.	0	5	0
Hodgson, J. L.	0	5	0
Maloney, S. H.	0	5	0
Turner, Mrs.	0	6	0
Ruthning, J.	0	5	0
Healey, W.	0	5	0
Black, J. and G.	0	5	0

	£	s	d
Hooper, G.	0	5	0
Dakers, R. A.	0	5	0
Sums under 5s.	0	2	0

Collected by Miss P. Campbell—

	£	s	d
Campbell, P.	0	2	6
Dudderly, J. W.	1	1	0
Golden, N.	0	5	0
Morrison, A.	0	5	0
A Friend	0	5	0
Sterling, J.	0	10	0
A Friend	0	5	0
Hume, W. C.	0	10	0
Weall, Mrs.	0	5	0
Hodgson, R.	0	2	6
Munro, A. and D.	0	10	6
Bennett, G. F.	0	5	0

WARWICK.

	£	s	d
Overend, J. and A.	5	5	0
Taylor, Dr.	1	1	0
Margetts, Dr.	1	1	0
Hubert, H.	1	1	0
Horwitz and Co., J.... ...	1	0	0
Everden, S.	1	0	0
McDougall, M. S., Lynd-			
hurst	1	0	0
Dwyer, T. A.	0	10	6
Brown and Wilson ...	0	10	6
Crouton and Irvine... ...	0	10	6
Nunn, J.	0	10	0
Benjamin and Co., H. ...	0	10	0
Glispie, L. G.	0	10	0
Wilkins, R.	0	10	0
Matthews, Rev. J.	0	10	0
Aland, R.	0	10	0
Croaker, G. T....	0	10	0
Ross, J. R.	0	10	0
Isambert, C. J....	0	10	0
Thompson, E.	0	10	0
Hayes, W. H.	0	10	0
Hodgson and Watkinson...	0	10	0
Bellemy, R. T.	0	10	0
Milford, S. N. Toulburra	0	10	0
Clipsham, Rev. P.	0	10	0
Saunders, S.	0	10	0
Beeson, T....	0	7	0
Higgins, P.	0	5	0
A Friend	0	5	0
McDonald, M....	0	5	0
Conway, D.	0	5	0
Tullock, A.	0	5	0
Johnson, T. A....	0	5	0
Clark, D.	0	5	0
Morgan, A.	0	5	0

Chavasse, G. W. £0 5 0	De Boys, ... £0 5 0
Barth, C. 0 5 0	Fevre, H. 0 5 0
Grayson, F. 0 5 0	Prussong, Y. 0 5 0
Station Master... ... ... 0 5 0	Hoffman, P. 0 5 0
Grenier, W. 0 5 0	Millar, Mrs. 0 5 0
Ryan, J. 0 5 0	Sums under 5s... ... ... 0 12 0
Roggenkamp, C. 0 5 0	

SCHOOL FEES, AND PAYMENTS FOR CLOTHING.

Britcheno,... ... ... £3 10 0	Jones (Clothing) £0 8 6
Burnes, ... 10 0 0	Milroy, ... 5 0 0
Ditto, (Clothing)... ... 1 5 6	McDonald, ... 19 10 0
Booth, ... 7 10 0	Ditto, (Clothing)... ... 2 3 6
Bailey, (Clothing) 9 3 2	McLaughlin, ... 13 10 0
Butler, (Ditto)... ... ... 1 6 10	Ditto, (Clothing)... ... 2 16 0
Bull, (Ditto) 10 0 0	
	O'Neill, ... 12 10 0
Churchill,... ... ... 3 5 0	Osman, (Clothing) 0 8 6
Carter, ... 1 0 0	
Clapham, (Clothing) ... 0 8 0	Provost, ... 2 10 0
	Ditto, (Clothing)... ... 1 0 0
Dawson, ... 7 10 0	Pike, (Ditto) 2 2 6
Ditto, (Clothing) 3 4 6	
Darcey, ... 3 0 0	Queensland Government .. 80 0 0
Ditto, (Clothing)... ... 0 3 6	
Durham, ... 5 0 0	Rogan, ... 3 15 0
Ditto, (Clothing) 3 12 6	Ditto, (Clothing) 2 15 0
	Raff, ... 14 0 0
Farr,... ... ... 20 0 0	Ditto, (Clothing)... ... 6 0 0
Fellew, ... 10 0 0	Ritchie, (Ditto) 6 0 0
Fitzpatrick, (Clothing) ... 1 10 0	
	Smith, ... 10 0 0
Gilbert 25 0 0	Smails, (Clothing) 0 15 9
Ditto, (Clothing) 0 17 6	
Golding (Ditto) 3 14 0	Tasmanian Government ... 40 0 0
Griffiths, (Ditto) 2 0 0	Todd, (Clothing) 0 8 0
Glode, (Ditto) 6 0 0	Tyrrell, (Ditto) 5 10 0
	Thomas, (Ditto) 6 0 0
Hall,... ... ... 9 0 0	
Ditto, (Clothing)... ... 0 14 0	Wilshire, ... 26 10 0
Hudson, ... 30 0 0	Ditto, (Clothing)... ... 0 14 0
Hill, (Clothing) 4 10 6	Wilbow, ... 6 5 0
Hicks, (Ditto) 3 17 1	Ware, (Clothing) 4 9 2
Jones, ... 8 0 0	

MISCELLANEOUS DONATIONS AND SERVICES.

Rendered during the year from the following, and thankfully acknowledged:—

Barker, Mrs., Newtown, Toys, &c.

Barker, F. J., *Illustrated London News*, *Punch*, &c.

Baptist, John, Esq., Flowers at different times.

Britchens, Mr., Vegetables at different times.

Colonial Sugar Works Company, Casks of Treacle.

Civil Service Musical Society, Free admission to Concerts for Blind Pupils.

Cameron, Mrs. E. W., Oranges.

Dickson, Mrs., Case of Oranges.

Davis, Mrs., Newtown, Boots for Blind.

Dangar, F. H., Esq., Christmas Treat.

Dean, Miss, £1 for Books and Toys.

Elsen, Mr., Brisbane, £1 to buy fruit for the Children.

Fache, Mrs., Cleveland House, Books for Library, Toys, &c., on two different occasions, and £2.

Fairfax, Mrs. C., Numbers of *Illustrated London News* and Music.

Fawnes, Rev. Mr., Tasmania, £1 for Toys.

Gibson, — Esq., £2 to buy Treat and Toys for the Children.

Goodlet, Mrs., Prizes for Needlework, &c., &c.

Griffiths, Mrs., Ashfield, Quantity of passion fruit.

Gratuitous copies of *Illustrated Sydney News*, *Australian Churchman*, and *Sydney Mail* from the Proprietors.

Hay, Lady, Picnic to all pupils and officers, Buns, lollies, butter and eggs, at different times.

Holt, Mrs., "The Warren," Buns for Good Friday.

Haig, Mrs., Monthly Number of *Old Jonathan*.

Henry, Mrs. James, Dentistry.

Hungerford, Rev. S., Books for Library.

Harrison, G. D., Collection and Assistance to the Collector in Brisbane.

Hopkins, W., Rockhampton, Assistance to Collector.

Joy, E., Esq., Donation of £2 for Drawing pupils.

Jeanneret, C. E., Esq., A free trip by steamer to Gladesville to pupils and friends.

Joubert, D. N., Esq., A free trip by steamer for pupils and friends to private residence of D. N. Joubert, Esq., Lane Cove.

Leeds, Mr., Orange, Case of Fresh Meat.

Love, Mrs., Parcels of lollies at different times.

Leigh, Mr., Ipswich, Assistance to Collector.

Levy, Mrs., Cakes, lollies, &c.

Lewington, Mitchell and Co., Donation of Thurms.

Moore, Mr. S., Castle Hill, Cases of fruit.

Milson, Mr., Free passages for Children and Officers to North Shore during Holidays.

Moses, Solomon, Lollies.

Metcalfe, Mrs. M., Vegetables, Tea-cakes, Fruit and Sweets.

Phillips, Mrs. Henry, Treat to Children of Buns, Cakes, Lollies, &c.

Rutter, J. J., Esq., Milton, Parcels of Books.

Sydney United Omnibus Company, Omnibus free of charge to Circular Quay and back.

Seymour, Mr., Donation of fish at different times.

Spencer, Mr., Pitt street, Admission free to Museum.

Smith, Mrs., Kurrajong, Case of Oranges.

Skeldon, Mrs. Henry, Brooklyn, U. S., America, £1 for Books and Toys.

Samuel, Hon. Saul, M.L.C., Tin of Lollies.

Slee, Mrs., Cakes, &c.

Sutherland, Hon. John, M.P., Free Train to Menangle Station for children on Easter Monday.

Taylor, Hugh, Esq., M.P., Picnic to Parramatta.

Threlkeld and Company, Tea and Sugar.

Taylor, Rev. R., Picnic to Parramatta with St. Stephen's School children.

Taylor, Mr., St. Paul's College, Case of Oranges.

Wigzell, Mr., Attendance monthly to cut children's hair.

List of work done since October 1877 to 1878.—

42 Dresses
12 Pinafores
15 Aprons
16 Drawers
13 Chemises
6 Night Dresses
6 Night Shirts
5 Crimean Shirts
18 Petticoats
3 Hoods
4 Vests

5 Coats
18 Trousers
33 Sheets
12 Table Cloths
64 Pillow Slips
18 Towels
30 Bed Covers
3 Stay Bodies
____
327 Articles.

Information and Directions relative to the Admission of Children to the Institution.

1. Applications must be in writing addressed to the Secretary, sent before the child is brought to the Institution, and should contain as full information as possible, the necessary forms can be obtained of the Hon. Secretary.

2. Pupils are admissible from any part of the colony of New South Wales, and under certain conditions, from Queensland, Tasmania, and New Zealand.

3. No child deficient in intellect, subject to fits, or unable to wash and dress itself, can be considered a fit subject for admission.

4. Children from seven to twelve years of age are eligible for admission, but in no case shall the age be above 15 years.

5. No order will be given by the Committee for a child's admission until the medical certificate has been obtained.

6. Children on entering the Institution are required to have two complete suits of clothing, for school or week-day wear, to be of dark colour, and a better suit for Sunday, and be provided with clothing (see list) by their parents or friends during their residence, each child must be provided with a Box or Trunk in which to keep clean clothing for use. If £5 is remitted the Committee will purchase outfit on admission.

7. Any amounts remitted to the Secretary for the purchase of clothing will be expended under the direction of the Committee of Management.

8. The fees payable in ordinary cases for the board, education, &c., of children in the Institution are:—£25 per annum; in special cases a lower scale of fees is adopted.

9. In the case of pauper children, a certificate of inability to pay any fee must be obtained from known individuals.

10. The fees are payable in advance, and date from the time of admission.

11. Children cannot be permitted to leave the Institution unless with the direct sanction and authority of the Committee.

12. In addition to the usual educational course the girls are taught household duties, and the boys out-door and other work.

13. The vacations are 5 weeks at Christmas, and 1 week at Mid-Winter, and it is essential that pupils should return to the Institution on the day fixed to commence duties after each vacation, and with their clothing clean and in proper order. See List.

14. The average term of Residence in the Institution is for Deaf and Dumb pupils 6 to 8 years, and for Blind pupils 3 to 5 years.

15. The Parents and Friends of children are admitted once a fortnight, on Thursdays, between the hours of 12 noon and 3 p.m.

16. The children are permitted to visit their friends once a month, on special application being made to the Committee.

17. Money orders should be made payable to the Secretary or Treasurer at the Head Office, Post Office, George-street, Sydney.

18. It is requested all communications be addressed to the undersigned,

ELLIS ROBINSON, *Hon. Secretary*,
at the Institution, or 486, George-street, Sydney.

NEW SOUTH WALES
Institution for the Deaf and Dumb and the Blind.
NEWTOWN ROAD.

The following quantity of Clothing is required for each child, to be supplied on its entering the Institution, which it is anticipated will, with a few additions and repairs, last for twelve months :—

For Boys.

2 Suits for week-day wear
1 Suit for Sunday ditto
4 Shirts, day—white or crimean
2 Ditto night
6 Pairs Socks
2 Caps or Felt Hats
6 Collars
6 Handkerchiefs
2 Pairs Cotton Braces
2 Neckties
1 Hair and 1 Tooth Brush
1 Rack and 1 Fine Tooth Comb
2 Pairs Boots

For Small Boys.

3 Holland Pinafores may be supplied.

For Girls.

3 Dresses for week-day wear
1 Dress for Sunday ditto
2 Petticoats, general use
1 Petticoat, Sunday ditto
6 Pairs Stockings or Socks
2 Hats
6 Plain Linen Collars or Frills
6 Handkerchiefs
1 Warm Jacket
6 Pairs Drawers
2 Pairs Stays or Bodices
3 Chemises
3 Night Dresses
6 Pinafores or Aprons
1 Rack and 1 Fine Tooth Comb
1 Hair and 1 Tooth Brush
2 Pairs Boots.

Each child to be provided with a Box or Trunk in which to keep Clothing when clean for use. The Clothing in all cases must be Dark Coloured. The Girls' Dresses may be Print for Summer wear, and Alpaca, Wincey, or similar material for Winter wear.

Boys' suits should be of Dark Coloured washing Tweed or other similar material. (Drill suits are not to be worn ; if sent, parents must provide for having them washed.)

ELLIS ROBINSON,

March 31, 1873.   *Honorary Secretary.*

SPECIAL INFORMATION.

———◆———

"The object of this Institution is the educating, and mainten-
ance whilst so doing, of Deaf and Dumb or Blind children, from
the age of seven years ; to enable them to earn their own living,
make them useful members of society, and prevent them becoming,
as they would in most cases, a burden upon public charity in after
years."

The Institution is open to Subscribers and other Visitors daily
—Saturdays, Sundays, and holidays accepted,—from 2 to 4 p.m.

The Parents and Friends of children are admitted once a
fortnight, on Thursdays, between the hours of 12 noon and 3 p.m.

The children are permitted to leave the Institution to visit
their friends once a month, on special application being made to
the Committee.

Forms and all particulars for the admission of pupils into
the Institution, and copies of the Rules and Regulations, can be
obtained of the Honorary Secretary.

Subscriptions and Donations will be thankfully received and
acknowledged by the Treasurer, the Secretary, or at the Institution. Donations or Bequests of over £100 are placed to a Perpetual Subscribers' Fund.

The Meetings of Committee are held on the Second Monday
in each month, at 4 o'clock p.m. The Ladies Visiting Committee
meet at the Institution, on the last Friday in the month, at 3
o'clock in the Winter, and half past 3 o'clock in the Summer
months.

Donations of Meat, Vegetables, Fruit (Fresh and Preserved,)
are thankfully received and acknowledged ; also clothing and
Materials for the same will be thankfully accepted.

The cost of passages to and from the Institution must be paid
by the Friends of the pupils. The Committee having no Fund for
this purpose.

All communications to be addressed to Ellis Robinson,
Honorary Secretary, at the Institution, or 486, George-street,
Sydney.

Money orders should be made payable to the Secretary or
Treasurer at the Head Office, Post Office, St. Martin's, Sydney.

It is highly necessary that the Parents or Friends of children notify to the Secretary any change of Residence in case of
illness, or other cause requiring immediate communication.

No._____

NEW SOUTH WALES
Institution for the Deaf & Dumb, & the Blind.

———o———

COPY OF FORM OF RECOMMENDATION FOR ADMISSION.

1. State Christian Name and Surname, Age, and Religion of the Child recommended for admission, and Native Place..	
2. State Christian Names and Surnames of the Father and Mother, also trade or calling, and present residence.....................	
3. State circumstances of the case ; also as to the amount that the Parents or Friends are able and willing to contribute towards the maintenance and education of the Child, and what security can be offered that such payments will be duly made........................	

Signature of two Subscribers to the Institution.......... { 1_____
                      { 2_____

Signature of Clergyman or Magistrate of the District in { 3_____
which the Child resides......

*Dated this*_____ *day of*_____187

HISTORICAL STATEMENT of Candidate for Admission.

————o————   *No.*_____

DEAF AND DUMB CHILDREN.

————♦————

1. Name and Sex ... ...
2. Age and date of Birth... ... ...
3. Religion of Parents ... ...
4. Native place... ... ...
5. Usual Residence ... ...
6. Been afflicted from birth ... ...
7. Affliction hereditary ; i.e., by direct transmission from the Parents ? ...
8. Are any other members of the family or relatives of the Parents similarly afflicted ? ... ...
9. Is the affliction single or double ? ...
10. Has the single or double affliction always been present ?... ... ...
11. Is the power to hear sounds entirely absent ? ... ...
12. Is the power to utter articulate sounds entirely absent ? ... ...
13. Has Child suffered from fright, grief, or other emotional causes ? ... ...
14. Has Child suffered from fits of any kind, fever, palsy, or injury to head or spine ? ... ...
15. Has Child had Measles, Whooping Cough, or Scarlet Fever, and been vaccinated ?... ... ...
16. Are the Parents in any degree related, if so, what is their consanguinity ? ...
17. Does the Mother attribute the affliction to any circumstance occuring during her pregnancy ? ... ...
18. State condition of intellect ? ... ...
19. Is there any malformation of the interior of the mouth and throat ? ...
20. State any peculiarities of stature, bodily configuration, &c... ... ...
21. Are the Parents intemperate and profligate ? ... ...
22. Are any other children similarly afflicted known to the Parents as resident in their neighbourhood ? ...
23. How many other Children are there in family besides the Candidate ? ...
24. Are both Parents alive ? ... ...

Date of Admission........................... Date of Leaving...........................

HISTORICAL STATEMENT of Candidate for Admission.

———o———

BLIND CHILDREN. _No._ ____

———o———

1. Name and Sex of Candidate? ... ...
2. Age and date of birthday? ... ...
3. Religion of Parents? ... ...
4. Native place? ... ...
5. Present Residence? ... ...
6. Been afflicted from birth if not at what age? ... ...
7. Affliction hereditary; i.e., by direct transmission from Parents? ... ...
8. Are any other members or relatives of the family similarly afflicted? ... ...
9. Is there any other defect of the senses?
10. Sight entirely Gone? ... ...
11. If from accident or disease, describe the circumstances connected with the origin of the Blindness? ... ...
12. Has any Surgical Operation been performed for the relief of the Blindness?
13. Has child suffered from fright, grief, or other emotional causes?... ... ...
14. Has child suffered from fits of any kind, fever, palsy, or any injury to the head, face, or spine? ... ...
15. Has child had Measles, Whooping Cough, or Scarlet Fever, and been Vaccinated? ... ...
16. Are the Parents in any degree Related, what is their Consanguinity? ... ...
17. Does the Mother attribute the affliction to any circumstance occuring during her Pregnancy? ... ...
18. State condition of intellect? ... ...
19. Any malformation of interior of mouth or throat? ... ...
20. State any peculiarities of Stature, Bodily Configuration, &c. ... ...
21. Are the Parents intemperate or profligate?... ... ...
22. Are any other children similarly afflicted, known to the Parents as resident in the neighbourhood? ...
23. How many other children are there in the family? ... ...
24. Are both Parents alive? ... ...

Date of Admission........................ Date of Leaving........................

MEDICAL CERTIFICATE.

I certify that I have this day examined...and have found...........in good bodily health, and free from cutaneous and contagious disorders. I consider...........a fit subject for admission to the Institution. Date....................18......

..Honorary Medical Officer.

FORM OF A BEQUEST

TO THE

New South Wales Institution for the Deaf, and Dumb, and the Blind.

I give and bequeath unto *A. B. (or unto my said Executors—or my said Trustees as the case may be) the sum of*..............*upon trust to pay out of my Personal Estate to the Treasurer for the time being of "The New South Wales Institution for the Deaf and Dumb, and the Blind" such sum as a donation to the said Institution.*

The following is the proper attestation to a Will :—

Signed by the above-named testator as and }
for his last Will in our presence who }
in his presence at his request and in } *(Signatures and Addresses.)*
the presence of each other have sub- }
scribed our names as witnesses. }

All Legacies and Donations of £50 and upwards are now placed to credit of a Perpetual Subscribers Fund as an Endowment.

TABULAR STATEMENT OF NAMES &c., of CHILDREN who have been Pupils of the Institution

from the Foundation 1860, until September, 1878.

DEAF AND DUMB CHILDREN.

No.	Name.	Age on Admission.	Religion.	Where Received from.	Date of Admission.	Date of Leaving.	Other Children in family.	Remarks.
1	Lorsey, Patrick	...	Roman Catholic	Sydney, N.S.W.	...	...		Apprentice to a Shoemaker.
2	Thorp, Joseph	...	Ditto	Ditto	...	...		
3	Hagen, Felix	14	Ditto	Ditto	1860	...		Died.
4	Patterson, Henry	...	Protestant	Shoalhaven	...	...		Taken to Benevolent Asylum.—Idiotic.
5	Lentz, Anne	...	Ditto	Sydney	...	...		Only a short time a pupil.
6	Hurst, Susan	14	Ditto	Ditto	1860	...		Returned to friends.
7	Poulton, William	...	Ditto	Ditto	1860	1862		Gone to a trade.
8	Carmichael, Edward	11	Roman Catholic	Ditto	1860	...		Went to Scotland.
9	Bridgement, Annie	4	Protestant	Ditto	1860 Feb.	1864	Most of these Children were received into the Institution on opening. From the length of time elapsed it is difficult to obtain information about them.	Gone to a trade.
10	Plowright, Selina	12	Ditto	Ditto	1860 Sept.	1863		Since died.
11	Pearson, Elizabeth	17	Ditto	Ditto	1860 June	1864		
12	Morrow, William	9	Ditto	Camperdown	Jan. 1860	1864		Gone to a trade—Bootmaker.
13	Logan, Thomas	10	Ditto	Sydney	May 1863	1866		
14	Murray, Richard	5	Roman Catholic	Ditto	Aug. 1863	1864		Gone to a trade—Engineer.
15	Mailley, Harriet	14	Protestant	Ditto	Jan. 1862	1864		
16	Keene, Lizzie	12	Roman Catholic	Ditto	1860	1867		Went to Brisbane.
17	Lynch, Deborah	8	Protestant	Ditto	...	1864		Returned to her friends.
18	Gleadhill, Mary Jane	14	Ditto	Picton	1863 April	1864		Living with friends in Victoria.
19	Hill, Emma	9	Ditto	Sydney	1860	1866		In service now.
20	Mailley, Richard	13	Ditto	Ditto	Jan. 1865	1865		Gone to a trade—Bootmaker.
21	Smith, Thomas	14	Ditto	Hinton, Hunter River	1860	1864		Labourer.
22	McLaughlin, Richard	15	Ditto	Warialda, N.S.W.	Feb. 1862 May	1864	...	Returned to his friends.
23	McLaughlin, Thomas	12	Ditto	Warialda, N.S.W.	1862	1864	...	Returned to his friends.
24	Lewis, William	13	Ditto	Pyrmont, Sydney	Oct. 1862 Dec.	1865	...	Absconded and since dead.
25	Hart, Elizabeth	16	Ditto	New Zealand	Feb. 1862 Mar.	1866	...	Returned to New Zealand.

No.	Religion	Where from	Date Admitted	Date Left	No.	Remarks
11	Roman Catholic	Sofala, N.S.W.	Dec. 1861	Dec. 1865	...	Returned to her friends.
11	Ditto	Appin	April 1861	June 1869	9	Ditto ditto.
7	Ditto	Sydney	Feb. 1862	Sep. 1865	4	Ditto ditto.
5	Unitarian	Parramatta	,, 1862	Oct. 1873	4	Ditto ditto. Farm Servant.
11	Protestant	Shellharbour	Aug. 1862	...1875	...	Went to a trade—Saddler.
10	Ditto	Richmond	Jan. 1862	June 1866	1	Was Idiotic & taken to an Asylum for Insane.
10	Ditto	Concord	Nov. 1864	Mar. 1865	4	Sent to Newcastle Institution for Imbeciles.
10	Ditto	Fitzroy Iron Mines	Feb. 1865	Feb. 1872	8	Pupil Teacher.
11	Ditto	Irish Town, N.S.W.	May. 1865	...	6	Gone to work at a Coal Mine.
13	Ditto	Newcastle, ditto	Nov. 1865	...1873	...	Returned to friends. Dressmaker.
16	Ditto	Wentworth, ditto	July 1865	Nov. 1868	4	,, ,,
13	Ditto	Nerigunda, ditto	July 1865	Jan. 1870	6	,, ,,
6	Roman Catholic	Broadwater, Nanoi R.	Dec. 1866	...	...	Married.
8	Protestant	Bathurst, N.S.W.	Jan. 1866	May 1869	4	Returned to her friends.
13	Ditto	Goulburn, ditto	Feb. 1866	...	1	Now in the Institution.
5	Ditto	Lachlan, ditto	May 1866	...	9	Pupil Teacher.
5	Ditto	Shellharbour, ditto	Aug. 1866	Sept. 1871	5	Returned to her friends.
15	Ditto	Newcastle, ditto	Sept. 1866	Nov. 1871	3	Gone to a trade—Shoemaker.
12	Ditto	Hobart Town, Tasmania	Nov. 1866	...	...	Ditto ditto—Tinsmith.
8	Ditto	Rockhampton, Queensld.	July 1867	...	5	Left the Institution.
18	Ditto	Sydney	Aug. 1867	Nov. 1875	8	Returned to friends.
10	Ditto	Windsor, N.S.W.	Jan. 1868	...	3	Returned to parents.
12	Ditto	King's Plains, Queensland	Sept. 1868	...	3	Taken away by his friends.
13	Hebrew	Sydney	Nov. 1868	...	4	Returned to Brisbane.
11	Roman Catholic	Ditto	April 1869	...	4	Returned to parents.
6	Protestant	Ipswich, Queensland	Jan. 1869	Dec. 1877	4	,, ,,
6	Ditto	Ditto, ditto	Feb. 1869	Aug. 1877	4	Now in the Institution.
6	Protestant	Sydney	April 1869	Nov. 1878	4	Left the Institution.
4	Ditto	Queanbeyan	,, 1869	...	4	Gone to a trade—Dressmaker.
8	Roman Catholic	Ditto	,, 1869	...	5	Ditto ditto.
9	Protestant	New England, N.S.W.	May 1869	Dec. 1876	1	Idiotic & removed to Asylum for Insane.
7	Ditto	Manning River	July 1869	June 1877	7	Returned to New Zealand.
7	Ditto	Sydney	Nov. 1866	Dec. 1866	4	Now in the Institution.
9	Ditto	Araluen	May 1869	Feb. 1877	10	Returned to friends.
5	Ditto	Auckland, New Zealand	... 1869	...	...	...
10	Ditto	Redfern, N.S.W.	Feb. 1869	Feb. 1877	...	...
	Ditto	West Maitland, N.S.W.	Oct. 1869	,, 1875		

TABULAR STATEMENT OF NAMES, &c.—Continued.

DEAF AND DUMB CHILDREN.—Continued.

No.	Name.	Age on Admission.	Religion.	Where Received from.	Date of Admission.	Date of Leaving.	Other Children in family.	Remarks.
63	Boulton, Adelaide Rosina	11	Protestant	McLeay River, N.S.W.	Jan. 1870	May 1871	3	Returned to her friends to Victoria.
64	Jessup, Emmeline	9	Ditto	Ryde, Parramatta River	„ 1870	...	6	Now in the Institution.
65	Chapman, Bridget	5	Ditto	Sydney	June 1870	...	2	„ „ „
66	Churchill, Emma Deborah	10	Ditto	Port McQuarie	Aug. 1870	...	7	Returned to friends. A Saddler.
67	Howe, Frederick	10	Ditto	Newtown, N.S.W.	Sep. 1870	Dec. 1875	1	„ „ returned to his friends.
68	Carpenter, John Thomas	7	Ditto	Ryde, Parramatta River	Oct. 1870	Nov. 1870	2	Idiotic and returned to his friends.
69	McDonald, Augustus John	8	Ditto	Concord, ditto	Jan. 1871	...	1	Now in the Institution.
70	Bridgement, Anna Elizab.	12	Ditto	Sydney	Feb. 1871	July 1874	4	Returned to her friends.
71	Britcheno, Halston Elizab.	7	Ditto	Waterloo, N.S.W.	Mar. 1871	...	1	Now in the Institution.
72	Hurst, Herbert	6	Ditto	Wollongong	July 1871	Aug. 1877	4	Returned to Parents.
73	Durham, John Edwin	5	Ditto	Singleton, N.S.W.	Jan. 1871	...	4	Now in the Institution.
74	D'Arcy, William	7	Roman Catholic	Sydney	Feb. 1872	...	2	„ „
75	Arrell, Henry	11	Protestant	Brisbane, Queensland	Mar. 1872	Dec. 1876	6	Draughtsman Works Dep. Queensland Gov.
76	Smith, Henry Caulfield	9	Ditto	Newtown	Mar. 1872	„ 1877	6	Returned to friends.
77	Jordan, Eliza Jane	6	Ditto	Queanbeyan	April 1872	„ 1873	5	Idiotic—taken to Newcastle Asylum.
78	McLaughlen, Frank	12	Ditto	Goorah, N.S.W.	„ 1872	„ 1877	7	Returned to friends.
79	Cameron, Lachlan	9	Ditto	Goulburn	May 1872	„ 1877	6	„ „
80	Rodgers, Ellen	9	Roman Catholic	Coolac, N.S.W.	Sept. 1872	„ 1876	6	Returned to parents.
81	Goldsworthy, James	8	Protestant	Adelaide, S.A.	„ 1872	„ 1875	0	Returned to his friends.
82	Harriss, Laura Eva	9	Ditto	Wollonbi, N.S.W.	„ 1872	Dec. 1875	4	Returned to her friends.
83	White, Ida	5	Ditto	Merriwa, ditto	„ 1872	...	1	Died.
84	Wehrman, Adolph	9	Protestant	Ipswich, Queensland	„ 1872	...	1	Drowned.
85	Ruwald, Elizabeth Mary	10	Roman Catholic	Newcastle, N.S.W.	Feb. 1873	Jan. 1876	5	Returned to her friends.
86	Jones, Martha	8	Protestant	Clarence Town, ditto	„ 1873	...	4	Now in the Institution.
87	Jones, Annie	6	Ditto	Ditto ditto, ditto	„ 1873	...	4	„ „ „
88	Smith, Margaret	18	Ditto	South Creek, ditto	„ 1873	...	1	„ „ „
89	King, Margaret	9	Roman Catholic	Queensland	Aug. 1873	...	9	„ „ „
90	Ryan, Mary Anne	13	Ditto	Hobart Town, Tasmania	Nov. 1873	Nov. 1876	2	Returned to Tasmania.
91	Ransley, Clara	12	Protestant	„	June 1874	...	10	Now in the Institution.

No.	Name	Age	Religion	Native Place	Date Admitted	Date Left	Yrs.	Remarks
92	Fitzpatrick, James	6	Roman Catholic	Moruya, N.S.W.	Aug. 1871	…	3	Now in the Institution.
93	Wilbow, George	11	Protestant	Moonby, "	" 1874	…	3	"
94	Tyrrell, William	7½	Ditto	Armidale	Jan. 1875	…	5	"
95	Tyrrell, Joseph	4½	Ditto	Ditto	" 1875	…	5	"
96	Harrison, Herbert Cornish	7	Protestant	Brisbane, Queensland	Jan. 1875	…	3	"
97	Harrison, William Smith	6	Ditto	Ditto	" 1875	…	3	"
98	Barnes, Eliza	5	Ditto	Moonbi, N.S.W.	Feb. 1875	…	9	"
99	Bailey, Eliza Jane	10	Ditto	Fish River, Bathurst	" 1875	…	7	"
100	Osman, William Edward	7	Roman Catholic	Sydney	Mar. 1875	…	5	"
101	Haberling, Albert	12	Protestant	Rockhampton, Q.	April 1875	…	2	"
102	Jordan, Richard Mehegan	6	Ditto	Queanbeyan	April 1875	…	2	Has 2 Brothers inmates.
103	Northcote, Margaret Ann	7	Ditto	Brisbane	June 1875	…	6	Now in the Institution.
104	Cox, Thomas	10	Roman Catholic	Sydney	June 1875	Dec. 1876	3	Returned to parents.
105	King, Anne	7	Ditto	Queensland	July 1875	…	5	Has a Sister an inmate.
106	Reuter, C.	6	Protestant	Grafton	June 1875	…	7	Now in the Institution.
107	Dawson, Burt	12	Ditto	Denison Town, N.S.W.	Dec. 1876	…	4	Incapable of receiving Instruction.
108	McGillivray, Jane	14	Ditto	Kiama	Feb. 1876	Mar. 1876	3	Now in the Institution.
109	Prevost, Alice Maud	7	Ditto	Newcastle	Feb. 1876	…	5	Now in the Institution.
110	Pickard, Maria	7	Ditto	St. Leonards	Mar. 1876	April 1876	6	Idiotic. Returned to friends.
111	Begent, Laura Alice	7	Ditto	Sydney	June 1876	…	3	Now in the Institution.
112	McDonald, Robert	12	Ditto	Brisbane	May 1876	…	5	"
113	Phelps, Catherine M.	12	Roman Catholic	Sydney	Aug. 1876	…	4	"
114	Thompson, Thomas	12	Protestant	Rockhampton	Jan. 1877	…	3	"
115	Hall, Albert	9	Ditto	Manning River	"	…	4	"
116	Griffiths, Mary A.	10	Ditto	Tamworth	"	…	5	"
117	Wilshire, L. K.	9	Ditto	Berrima	Feb.	…	6	"
118	Ritchie, Jane	7	Ditto	Ipswich	July	…	5	"
119	Glode, August	11	Ditto	Queensland	"	…	4	"
120	Adams, Thomas	7	Ditto	Maneroo	Dec.	…	4	Returned to friends.
121	O'Neill, James	8½	Roman Catholic	Sydney	Oct.	…	4	Now in the Institution.
122	O'Keefe, Patrick	9	Ditto	Queensland	Feb. 1878	…	4	"
123	Booth, Fletcher Samuel	7½	Protestant	Smithfield, near Mudgee	March	…	2	"
124	Webb, James Dudley	7½	Ditto	Penrith	April	…	4	"
125	Northcote, William A.	8	Ditto	Warwick, Queensland	Oct.	…	4	Has a Sister an inmate.
126	Massey	7	Roman Catholic	Brisbane	"	…		"
127	Ryan, Mary Jane	10	Ditto	Toowoomba, Queensland	"	…	12	"
128	Leeder, Archibald Thomas	10	Ditto	Rockhampton, "	"	…	5	Now in the Institution.

TABULAR STATEMENT OF NAMES, &c.—Continued.

BLIND CHILDREN.

No.	Name.	Age on Admission.	Religion.	Where received from.	Date of Admission.	Date of Leaving.	other Children in family.	Remarks.
1	Adams, Edmund	13	Protestant	Newtown	Mar. 1869	Dec. 1870	11	Returned to his friends.
2	Worsley, Sarah Ann	10	Ditto	Camperdown	"	Mar. 1874	3	" her "
3	Saunders, John W.	8	Ditto	Iccly Copper Mines	"		1	Now in the Institution. Chair caner.
4	Whannell, James A.	8	Ditto	Sydney, N.S.W.	Aug.	Jan. 1870	3	Left the Colony.
5	Driscoll, John B.	13	Ditto	Rockhampton	Sept.	" 1874	3	Gone to a Trade.
6	McQuade, Susan Teresa	5	Roman Catholic	Sydney	Nov.		2	Now in the Institution.
7	Ellis, John Frank	10	Protestant	Singleton, N.S.W.	Jan. 1870	Dec. 1876	3	Caner. Returned to parents.
8	Allison, George Robert	8	Ditto	Brisbane, Queensland.	May 1871	July 1877	2	Returned to parents.
9	Todd, Mary Jane	5	Ditto	Rockhampton	Jan. "		0	Now in the Institution.
10	Kluge, Mary Anne	6	Roman Catholic	Grenfel, N.S.W.	June "		2	"
11	Hicks, Mary Ann	6	Protestant	Bowen, Queensland	Sept. 1872		1	"
12	Smith, Anne	10	Ditto	Braidwood	" "	Mar. 1877	4	"
13	Grube, John	9	Ditto	Sydney	July 1873	Jan. 1874	4	Died.
14	Everingham, Henrietta	12	Ditto	Windsor, N.S.W.	" "	June 1877	7	Returned to parents.
15	Read, Sophia Jane	12	Ditto	Sydney	Jan. 1874	Nov. 1877	1	
16	Mereer, Thomas	9	Ditto	Tasmania	July "	"	0	Now in the Institution.
17	Pike, James Henry	9¼	Ditto	Newcastle	April 1875		4	"
18	Hill, Bell Leonard	12	Ditto	Cobbora	Feb. 1876		6	"
19	Milroy, Matthew	10	Ditto	Newtown	April "		6	"
20	Hudson, Louisa E.	12	Ditto	Paddington	Aug. "		6	"
21	Gilbert, David	16	Ditto	Newcastle	Feb. 1877		7	"
22	Usherwood, Alice	8	Ditto	Tasmania	Feb. "		8	"
23	Rogan, James	12	Roman Catholic	Parkes	April "		4	"
24	Townsend, William	12	Protestant	Brisbane	July "		0	"
25	Fellew, Thomas Henry	16	Ditto	Sydney	Oct. "		6	"
26	Lethbridge, John Dennis	13½	Roman Catholic	Warwick, Queensland.	" 1878		7	"

NOTE.—A reference to the tables will show that 154 Children, 128 Deaf and Dumb, and 26 Blind, have been received. Of these 84 have left to return to their friends and homes. 6 were found to be Idiotic, and beyond the influence of education, and were removed to Asylums for Insane, one died. 70 now remain. In 15 of the families are two or more deaf and dumb. 117 of the children belong to New South Wales, 29 from Queensland, 2 New Zealand, 6 Tasmania, and South Australia.

The receipt of the Reports of the undermentioned Institutions is thankfully acknowledged :—

Ulster Society for the Deaf and Dumb and the Blind.
London Association for Promoting Welfare of the Blind.
Liverpool School for Indigent Blind.
Glasgow Asylum for Blind.
British Asylum for Deaf and Dumb Females, London.
Edinburgh Institution for Deaf and Dumb.
Victorian Institution for Deaf and Dumb.
Victorian Institution for the Blind.
New York Institution for Deaf and Dumb.
New York State Institution for the Blind, U. S.
Proceedings Second Convention of American Instructors of the Blind.
New York State Institution for the Blind, Trustees and Officers Report.
Arkansas Institute for the Education of the Blind, U. S.
Illinois Institution for the Blind, Jacksonville, U. S.
Pensylvania Working Home for Blind Men, U. S.
Missouri Institution for the Blind, U. S.
Report American Printing House for the Blind, U. S.
Minnesota Institution for Deaf and Dumb and Blind, U. S.
Kentucky Asylum for the Blind, U. S.
Georgia Academy for the Blind, U. S.
Bristol Asylum and School of Industry for the Blind.
California Institution for Deaf and Dumb and the Blind.
Maryland Institution for the Blind, Baltimore, U. S.
Maryland Institution for Deaf Mutes, Mass.
American Asylum for Deaf and Dumb, Hartford, U. S.
Tennessee School for Blind.
Clarke Institution for Deaf Mutes, Northampton, U. S.
North Carolina Institution for the Deaf and Dumb and the Blind.
Ohio Institution for the Education of the Blind.
Institution for the Learning of the Blind, Texas.
L' Instituto dei Serdo—Muti di Sienna.
Ontario Institution for the Education of the Blind, Toronto.
Deaf and Dumb Christian Association for Ireland.
Association for Oral Instruction of the Blind.
Dublin Protestant Association for the adult Deaf and Dumb.
The General Institution for the Blind, Edgebaston, England.
Columbia Institution for Deaf and Dumb, Washington.
West Virginia Institution for Deaf and Dumb and the Blind.

JOSEPH COOK & CO.,

PRINTERS.

SYDNEY.

The Dumb Child.—(ANONYMOUS.)

She is my only girl,—
I asked for her as some most precious thing,
For all unfinish'd was love's jewell'd ring
    "Till set with this soft pearl.
The shade that time brought forth I could not see
So pure, so perfect, seem'd the gift to me.

Oh! many a soft old tune
I used to sing into that deaden'd ear
And suffer'd not the lightest footstep near
    Lest she might wake too soon;
And hush'd her brothers' laughter while she lay;
Ah! needless care—I might have bid them play!

'Twas long ere I believed
That this one daughter might not speak to me:
Waited and watch'd, (God knows how patiently),
    How willingly received.
Vain love was long the untiring nurse of faith
And tended hope until it starved to death.

Oh! if she could but hear
For one short hour, that I her tongue might teach
To call me "Mother," in her broken speech
    That thrills the mother's ear!
Alas! These sealed lips never may be stirred
To the deep music of that lovely word.

My heart it sorely tries
To see her kneel with such a reverent air
Beside her brothers at their evening prayer:
    Or lift those earnest eyes
To watch our lips, as though our words she knew,
Then move her own, as she were speaking too.

I've watched her looking up,
To the bright wonder of an evening sky,
With such a depth of meaning in her eye,
    That I could almost hope
The struggling soul would burst its binding cords,
And the long pent-up thought flow forth in words.

The song of bird and bee,
The chorus of the breezes, streams, and groves,
All the great music to which nature moves,
    Are wasted melody
To her,—the world of sound a tuneless void,
While even silence hath its charm destroyed.

Her face is very fair
Her blue eyes beautiful,—of finest mould
Her soft white brow, o'er which in waves of gold
    Ripples her shining hair;
Alas! this lovely temple seal must be,
For He who made it hear ... ... a ter-key.

Wills He the mind within
Should from earth's babble-d noise be kept free,
Even that lisp still small voice ... and step might be
    Heard at its inner shrine.
Through that deep hush'd soul with clearer thrill,
The sound I grieve? Oh! murmuring heart be still.

She seems to have a sense
Of quiet gladness in her noiseless play;
She has a pleasant smile, a gentle way,
    Whose voiceless eloquence
Touches all hearts, though I had once the fear
That even her father would not care for her.

Thank God! it is not so:
And when his sons are playing merrily,
She comes and leans her head upon his knee,
    Oh! at such times I know,
By the full eye, and tone subdued and mild,
How his heart yearns over his silent child.

And God in love doth give
To her defect a beauty of its own;
And we a deeper tenderness have shown
    Through that for which we grieve:
Yet shall the soul be melt'd from the ear,
Yea, and my voice shall fill it,—but not here!

MANUAL ALPHABET.

Double Hand.

A a	B b	C c	D d	E e
F f	G g	H h	I i	J j
K k	L l	M m	N n	O o
P p	Q q	R r	S s	T t
U u	V v	W w	X x	Y y
Z z	Good	Bad	& &	Equal

CLEMENT & NYPP

www.ingramcontent.com/pod-product-compliance
Lightning Source LLC
Chambersburg PA
CBHW021513090426
42739CB00007B/597